Indigenous Archives in Postcolonial Contexts

Indigenous Archives in Postcolonial Contexts revisits the definition of a record and extends it to include memory, murals, rock art paintings and other objects.

Drawing on five years of research and examples from Zimbabwe, Botswana and South Africa, the authors analyse archives in the African context. Considering issues such as authentication, ownership and copyright, the book considers how murals and their like can be used as extended or counter archives. Arguing that extended archives can reach people in a way that traditional archives cannot and that such archives can be used to bridge the gaps identified within archival repositories, the authors also examine how such archives are managed and authenticated using traditional archival principles. Presenting case studies from organisations such as Gay and Lesbian Memory in Action Archives (GALA) and heritage projects such as the Makgabeng Open Cultural Museum, the authors also analyse Indigenous family praises and songs and explore how such records are preserved and transmitted to the next generation.

Indigenous Archives in Postcolonial Contexts demonstrates how the voices of the marginalised can be incorporated into archives. Making an important contribution to the effort to decolonise African archives, the book will be essential reading for academics and students working in archival studies, library and information science, Indigenous studies, African studies, cultural heritage, history and anthropology.

Mpho Ngoepe is a professor of information science and the Executive Director of Library and Information Services at the University of South Africa (Unisa). He was previously the Head of Information Science at the same institution. He worked for several organisations, including the National Archives of South Africa and the Auditor-General of South Africa. His research interests include archives, libraries, records management, indigenous archives, authentication, oral history, literature, and archival theories.

Sindiso Bhebhe is a post doctoral research fellow at the University of South Africa (Unisa). He holds a PhD in Information Science from Unisa. He has previously worked for the National Archives of Zimbabwe, and the National University of Science and Technology in Zimbabwe. His research interests include oral history, indigenous archives, and digital records management.

Indigenous Archives in Postcolonial Contexts
Recalling the Past in Africa

Mpho Ngoepe and Sindiso Bhebhe

LONDON AND NEW YORK

First published 2024
by Routledge
4 Park Square, Milton Park, Abingdon, Oxon OX14 4RN

and by Routledge
605 Third Avenue, New York, NY 10158

Routledge is an imprint of the Taylor & Francis Group, an informa business

© 2024 Mpho Ngoepe and Sindiso Bhebhe

The right of Mpho Ngoepe and Sindiso Bhebhe to be identified as authors of this work has been asserted in accordance with sections 77 and 78 of the Copyright, Designs and Patents Act 1988.

All rights reserved. No part of this book may be reprinted or reproduced or utilised in any form or by any electronic, mechanical, or other means, now known or hereafter invented, including photocopying and recording, or in any information storage or retrieval system, without permission in writing from the publishers.

Trademark notice: Product or corporate names may be trademarks or registered trademarks, and are used only for identification and explanation without intent to infringe.

British Library Cataloguing-in-Publication Data
A catalogue record for this book is available from the British Library

ISBN: 978-1-032-23502-8 (hbk)
ISBN: 978-1-032-23503-5 (pbk)
ISBN: 978-1-003-27798-9 (ebk)

DOI: 10.4324/9781003277989

Typeset in Times New Roman
by Newgen Publishing UK

Contents

List of figures vi
Acknowledgements vii
Foreword viii

Prologue: reimagining indigenous archives 1

1 Conceptualisation and recontextualisation of indigenous archival constructs 8

2 Decolonisation or (re)Africanisation of archives? 39

3 Authentication of indigenous archives 65

4 Ownership, copyright, and 'copyleft' of indigenous archives 82

5 Decolonisation and (re)Africanisation in action: a case study of community memory practices 95

6 Sustainable structures for indigenous archives in the postcolonial context 119

Epilogue: reflections and reflexivity 137

Index *143*

Figures

1.1	Rock art paintings by the San people	21
1.2	Rock art paintings by the Bantu-speaking people	22
1.3	Mural of Barolong kings	24
1.4.1	Mural of mayors of the City of eThekwini	25
1.4.2	Mural of the kings who ruled the Zulu nation from 1818 to present	26
1.5	Mural of late King Lobengula of the Ndebele nation in Zimbabwe	27
1.6	Mural of the daily activities of an ancient village in Mexico	28
1.7	The Comrades Marathon Hall of Honour	30
3.1	Blouberg-Makgabeng-Senwabarwana cultural festival	72

Acknowledgements

We visited many sites, investigating the contents of this book, and many people contributed in one way or another, especially those who provided family praises and their time to be interviewed. For this we are grateful to many people, including Mmasana Ngoepe and Mmasebatana Ramoroka (may her soul rest in eternal peace) and other elders of Makgabeng for providing family praises through oral tradition before they departed such as Mmaleasara Ngoepe, Mmanoko wa Ijone, and Venus Ramoroka, as well as Bhebhe and Dube clan for passing the word of mouth through the generational praise poetry. Dr Tlou Setumu, for many discussions we had over indigenous archives, as well as his writings on the subject. Mr Fortune Mabeba, the owner of Makgabeng Lodge, for always arranging the tours to the rock art paintings. Keval Harris, the Director of GALA queer archive and Linda Chernis, GALA Queer archive coordinator. Prof Samuel Mojapelo and Ms Onkutlwile Mere, for providing us with some of the pictures of the sites that we could not visit. Ms Alicia Bernard, for taking us on a tour of the history of Mexico and to one of the murals depicting early periods in Mexico (as we were able to compare the information we obtained in southern Africa and other regions of the world). Dr Daniel Mosako, for being helpful in interpreting murals as archives. Sello Hatang for writing the foreword of this book. Lastly, to Dr James Lowry for his valuable inputs to the book from proposal stage to publication. To those who opted to remain anonymous, we thank you.

Foreword

In a dialogue with Verne Harris about *Archives, Identity and Place: What it (might) Mean(s) to Be an African Archivist*, which was published in *ESARBICA* Journal issue 19 of 2000, we questioned why a conference hosted in an African country discussed nothing about indigenous African archives. That was an opportunity for African archivists gathered in Zanzibar to deliberate on how to transform, refigure and re-imagine archives, the practice of which in sub-Saharan Africa is still shaped and sharpened by the Western canons. As there was nothing distinctively about African or regional about the discourse at the conference, we thought the opportunity was missed.

The authors of this book had the same question about fifteen years later, in 2015, which culminated in the production of *Indigenous Archives in Postcolonial Contexts: Recalling the Pasts*. As a result, I am both excited and honoured to write the foreword to this book. This book is long overdue, at least from my conversation with Harris and it serves as a springboard for further debate on the decolonisation and (re)Africanisation of archives. This may pose a challenge to the narrow Eurocentric definitions of what constitutes a record or archive. The book classifies oral tradition as archives based on family praises and nomenclature. Africans can, in fact, trace their roots and family trees through family praises. Furthermore, the authors classify African rock art paintings and murals as archives. The authors' key questions include: What is an African archive, and how can it be revived? Is it necessary for this African archive to be kept on Eurocentric archival pedestals? This second question is very relevant and interesting in the discourse of the epistemic erasure of Indigenous African archival repositories because it calls for these to be recognised as independent and appreciated as equal to Western ways of archiving.

Another issue raised in this book is how African archives can be authenticated, as the question of who said what in oral history has always been taken seriously in Africa. This is because, as with blockchain technology, the distribution of the deceased's estate was based on the departed's last word of mouth with witnesses available. As a result, Africans developed systems for authenticating oral history records. Even though there were established systems of African kingship and chieftainship succession, the last word of mouth of the dying king or chief was taken seriously; thus, the importance of authenticating these records. This book delves into the topic of decolonisation, which has taken the global south by storm. It calls into question some of the global south's decolonisation approaches, labelling them as just perpetuations of epistemicides against African ways of knowing. Many African scholars, for example, are questioning the use of oral history as a complementary archival decolonisation strategy to fill what they call gaps left by Eurocentric written archives. The book then appears to advocate for the adoption of community archives as centres of African archival excellence, which will influence the prioritisation of African ways of knowing.

My heartfelt congratulations to the authors, Professor Mpho Ngoepe and Dr Sindiso Bhebhe, for producing this book and reminding those of us who work in memory space that there is still much work to be done in rescuing the African ways of archiving that were so prevalent prior to colonisation by the Empire and its imperialist forces. The book is a gentle call for us in the global south to guard against the isms that have destroyed African epistemologies, including African ways of archiving. African voices and indigenous archives are also crucial because they can contribute to solutions to grand societal challenges.

Sello Hatang
Former CEO: Nelson Mandela Foundation

Prologue
Reimagining indigenous archives

This book was conceptualised during the 23rd Eastern and Southern Africa Regional Branch of the International Council on Archives (ESARBICA) biennial conference, hosted by the National Archives of Zimbabwe from 8 to 12 June 2015, at the Elephant Hotel in Victoria Falls, Zimbabwe. During the conference, we had a tête-à-tête about the concept of indigenous archives, which was missing from the proceedings. The private discussion was sparked by the fact that the theme of the conference held in Africa was "archives use, abuse, and underutilisation" while neglecting the use, abuse, and underutilisation of indigenous archives. As a result, we decided to co-author a paper, which turned out to be a student/supervisor relationship. We conducted research into indigenous archives between 2015 and 2022, with an emphasis on oral history. This culminated in Sindiso Bhebhe completing his PhD on the topic "Memorialising minority groups in post-independence Zimbabwe and South Africa: a critical analysis of oral history programmes" under the supervision of Mpho Ngoepe. We also co-authored five articles that were published in peer-reviewed journals during the process. These articles focused on oral history as archives and compelled us to dig deeper into the concept of indigenous archives, as we discovered innumerable gaps. We then agreed to focus on oral memory, rock art paintings, and murals as records that can be used for decolonising and (re)Africanising archives. This book is the result of such interrogation of indigenous archives. Examples in the book are based on practices from countries in southern Africa such as South Africa, Zimbabwe, and Botswana.

2 *Prologue: reimagining indigenous archives*

Indigenous societies, especially in African countries, use oral transmission, rock art paintings, murals, and other memory practices to store and transmit valuable information from generation to generation. Harris (2020) calls some of these types of records "ghosts of ancestors" and states that their voices need to be included in the national archival system to build an inclusive archive. However, these forms of records are veiled and hidden by colonial constructs of what a record is and can be, and what constitutes an archive. When such sources are considered records, it is often when they appear in the four media defined by archival legislation, that is, paper, electronic, microfilm, and audio-visual format. These premises set by the Western civilisation can limit the ability to deal holistically with cultural memory and can obscure and diminish the validity and value of pre-colonial memory practices and traces, especially in countries that have seen a sustained attempt to control and even eradicate native cultures. Yet, in various parts of the world, indigenous peoples are reasserting the primacy of their own archival practices and archives through the United Nations Declaration on the Rights of Indigenous Peoples (UNDRIP) and its associated mandates, which provide important mechanisms for indigenous people to assert and explore rights to the management and preservation of their heritage (Hodge, Nantel & Trainor, 2022; Faulkhead & Thorpe, 2017).

In Canada, for example, as reported in a reflection by Ngoepe (2022a), the 2015 Truth and Reconciliation Calls to Action and the subsequent response work by the Steering Committee on Canada's Archives indicate that the archival profession is necessarily evolving with the aim of an inclusive, community-based approach to archival practice. According to Hodge et al. (2022, p. 147), a

> contributing element to these changes to praxis must be a confrontation of all colonial and settler archival theory, such as Hilary Jenkinson's writing, that is often presented as foundational within archival education, and as a mainstay in our professional mythology.

The work of the Steering Committee on Canada's Archives highlights the evolving professional movement, which accentuates the need for an inclusive, community-based approach to archival praxis. This approach is seen as a way of including the voices of those previously marginalised in the archives. The authors do not see how Western canons can pave the way towards accommodating indigenous traditional knowledge, which is mostly transmitted orally.

In their paper titled 'Dedication: Archival and Indigenous Communities,' Faulkhead and Thorpe (2014, p. 3) contend that "Indigenous people's views, definitions, and understandings of archives are often different and more diverse than those emanating from traditionally based Western archival science." For example, as is the case in some African countries, indigenous peoples in Australia have a sense of managing archives in ways that encompass spiritual, emotional, and physical connections to records. As reported by Faulkhead and Berg (2010), the indigenous people of Australia share a belief in the connection between the land and the people. This is also the case with Africa, as an Afrocentric perspective puts more emphasis on human beings than materiality, which seems to be a Eurocentric perspective (Setumu, 2021).

The Canadian and Australian situations also ring true in southern African countries such as Botswana, Lesotho, Eswatini, Zimbabwe, and South Africa, albeit with some differences and variations. Archival commentators such as Tough (2012, p. 245) observed that "the colonial archives have excluded the voices of natives in their holdings." As a result of criticism like this, oral history programmes that incorporate indigenous knowledge systems are being advocated to fill the gaps created by colonial archives (Manungo, 2012). In order to address this perceived gap, oral history programmes, documentation of murals and rock paintings are now expanded to cater for the post-independence communities in countries such as Zimbabwe and South Africa. Therefore, in recalling the past by exploring indigenous archives in a postcolonial context, this book is one of the first major African contributions to that discourse.

Oral history has mainly been used as one way to integrate indigenous culture into the Western-dominant archival discourse in Africa and elsewhere, but it should be noted that it is not the only method. However, in public archives, especially in South Africa, Zimbabwe, Botswana, and other sub-Saharan countries, oral history is often seen as of secondary importance to records and may even be seen as a factor working against the practices of good record-keeping (Archival Platform, 2015). Many people consider the truth to be only in recorded form, while forgetting that the other way of indirectly accessing the past is through oral history and other forms of recording. This book challenges these ideas and shows that in both cases of recorded form and indigenous memory practices, what is regarded as truth entirely depends on the trust of the source. It should be noted that in many in the African traditions, a witness is always needed when performing most cultural activities, which is one of the principles of blockchain technology. For example, a person cannot negotiate a dowry on his own without accompanying delegates (Ngoepe, 2022b). Furthermore, African ancestors also wrote their stories and messages with pictures and symbols etched on stone, bones, or cave walls (Setumu, 2015). It would seem such murals on the rocks were not considered writing by Western standards.

The purpose of this book is to explore memory, murals, and rock art paintings as records, as well as their authentication, ownership, and copyright. The book discusses how murals and rock art paintings can be used as extended or counter-archives, and their long-term viability as archives. In terms of archiving, the book also looks at how colonial governments viewed Africans and their traditions. The colonialist archives are still steeped in and reflective of colonial society's history, and indigenous peoples are only mentioned in passing. Case studies where such archives have been created and preserved, such as the memorialisation of the lesbian, gay, bisexual, transgender, and intersex (LGBTI) communities at the Gay and Lesbian Memory in Action Archive in South Africa, are discussed. Special attention to how they have used oral history in memorialisation is used to demonstrate how indigenous archives operate or can work in a postcolonial context. Other case sites of murals and rock art paintings are cited through the book as examples.

This book argues that public depictions of archives through murals can serve as a source of information and leave an everlasting impression because these records are in open space and are seen by the public on a daily basis. Since murals occupy public space, archives depicted as murals are meant to be physically and freely accessible to the public. The Western method of archiving has been criticised because it caters only for the elite and those in power. However, as we argue in this book, indigenous peoples are not immune to this, as they also tend to perpetuate elitism through the recording of stories of those who are high in rank, such as kings and chiefs, with little to say about the more everyday aspects of societies. Finally, the book proposes a sustainable structure for such records as counter-archives, ensuring their independence without relying heavily on mainstream archives. It is essential to determine how indigenous archives can be sustained to restore and preserve hidden memories, as well as to ensure continuity in their management.

In recalling the past and exploring indigenous archives in postcolonial contexts, we reviewed literature on related topics. We also visited Makgabeng Open Cultural Museum, the Comrades Marathon route, rock art paintings, stone walls, KARA Heritage Village, Lotlamoreng Dam in Mahikeng, Tso-ro-tso San Development Trust, and other case study locations. Photographs were taken of murals and rock art paintings during the visits and some are included in this book. Interviews were also conducted with independent oral historians, heritage practitioners, artists, and archivists. Both interviews and a literature review were used in a case study of the Gay and Lesbian Memory Action (GALA). Furthermore, the authors participated in the feasts where crests were displayed, traditional songs were performed, and family praises were recited, thereby confirming the people's official history. In this regard, the authors' family praises and songs, in particular, were analysed to contribute content to the book. Other family praises were gleaned from published literature. Documents such as legislation on archives and heritage, especially in South Africa and Zimbabwe were analysed. In this regard, the National Archives and Records Service of South Africa Act (Act No. 43 of 1996), the National Heritage Council of South Africa Act (Act No. 11 of 1999), the Traditional Leadership and Governance Framework of South Africa Act (Act No. 41 of 2003), the National Heritage Resources of South Africa Act (Act No. 25 of 1999), the Traditional Leaders Act of Zimbabwe (Act No. 29 of 2001) and the Copyright and Neighbouring Rights Act of Zimbabwe (Act No. 26 of 2004) were analysed.

The book is divided into six chapters. The first chapter establishes the concepts and context of our work by justifying the need to revisit concepts of archive by exploring indigenous archives in a postcolonial context. This is accomplished by discussing the concepts of orality, mural, and rock art paintings as archives in indigenous knowledge systems. After discussing what constitutes archives in the first chapter, Chapter Two examines how colonial governments viewed Africans and their traditions in terms of archiving. The archives left by the colonialists are still steeped in colonial society's history, and indigenous people are only mentioned in passing. The third chapter discusses how the identified indigenous archives are traditionally authenticated. In addition, archival principles, and disruptive technologies like blockchain technology are explored to see if they can be used to authenticate these records. Chapter Four dissects issues of ownership, copyleft, and copyright in indigenous memory practises such as rock art paintings, murals, and orality. Chapter Five demonstrates how indigenous archives operate or can operate in a postcolonial context through a case study. Chapter Six proposes a sustainable structure for the identified records to function as counter-archives while remaining independent of mainstream archives. It is essential to determine how indigenous archives can be sustained in order to restore and preserve memories obscured by colonialism, as well as to ensure continuity in their management. Overall, the book presents strategies for restoring trust in indigenous archives and redressing past and ongoing harms associated with archival work.

References

Archival Platform. (2015). State of the archives: an analysis of South Africa's archival system, 2014.
Faulkhead, K. and Berg, J. (2010). *Power and passion: our ancestors return home*. Melbourne: Koorie Heritage Trust Inc.
Faulkhead, S. and Thorpe, K. (2017). Dedication: archives and indigenous communities. In A.J. Gilliland, S. McKemmish and A.J. Lau (Eds.), *Research in Archival Multiverse*, Clayton: Monash University, pp. 2–15.
Harris, V. (2020). *Ghosts of archive: deconstructive intersectionality and praxis*. London: Routledge.
Hodge, S., Nantel, S. and Trainor, C. (2022). Remnants of Jenkinson: observations on settler archival theory in Canadian archival appraisal discourse. *Archives and Records*, 43(2): 147–160.
Manungo, K. (2012). Oral history as captured by the National Archives of Zimbabwe over the years. In P. Ngulube (Ed.). *National Archives*

75@30: 75 years of archiving excellence at the National Archives of Zimbabwe. National Archives of Zimbabwe, pp. 64–67.

Ngoepe, M. (2022a). Reflections on "Remnants of Jenkinson: observations on settler archival theory in Canadian archival appraisal discourse." *Archives and Records*, 43(2): 164–165.

Ngoepe, M. (2022b). Neither prelegal nor nonlegal: oral memory in troubled times. *HTS Teologiese Studies/Theological Studies*, 78(3): 6.

Setumu, T. (2015). Inclusion of rural communities in national archival and records system: a case study of Blouberg-Makgabeng-Senwabarwana area. *Journal of South African Society of Archivists*, 48: 34–44.

Setumu, T. (2021). *Moletji: history of Batlhaloga of Moloto Kingdom.* Polokwane: Mak Herp.

Tough, A.G. (2012). Oral culture, written records and understanding the twentieth-century colonial archive: The significance of understanding from within. *Archival Science*, 12(3): 245–265. doi:10.100710502-011-9162-1

1 Conceptualisation and recontextualisation of indigenous archival constructs

Introduction

In the introductory remarks to his autobiography, Tlou Setumu (2011), an author and heritage consultant in the Limpopo province of South Africa, writes that the conquest and material dispossession of indigenous African communities led to the present miseries in every aspect of their lives. This is because, prior to colonialism, communities in Africa, as elsewhere, had their own ways of doing things, whether in education, law, politics, religion, culture, archiving, or other aspects of life. Indigenous communities boast arts, culture, and heritage forms such as languages, legends, histories, folktales, riddles, proverbs, music, dance, and crafts, as well as indigenous knowledge systems in politics, medicine, astronomy, and economy (Setumu, 2016). However, European countries subjugated these practices and systems and imposed their values and ways of life on Africa and other regions of the world. The systems of indigenous communities were either obliterated or prohibited from being formally practiced, which deprived indigenous systems of the opportunity to develop. Where such systems survived and were practiced, they were not recognised by the colonial governments. We grew up in communities that still value and practise indigenous knowledge systems and we are witness to some of the gaps that are direct results of colonialism. It should be noted that in other regions of the world, especially in Asian countries such as South Korea, North Korea, Japan, and China, indigenous knowledge systems survived (Buenavista, Wynne-Jones & McDonald, 2018). For example, the Annals of the Joseon Dynasty (1392–1910), which is called

DOI: 10.4324/9781003277989-2

"Joseon Wangjo Sillok," is one of the most important historical documents in Korea and has been registered as a Memory of the World by the United Nations Educational, Scientific and Cultural Organization. The same cannot be said about indigenous archives of many African countries.

One of the most striking consequences of the European colonisation of Africa was the loss of identity and indigenous knowledge systems. Prior to colonialism, African communities and kingdoms built their societies around people, giving rise to the philosophy of Ubuntu (Humanity), in which a common allegiance to leadership was paramount. Ubuntu is an African philosophy that emphasises the essential human virtues of compassion and humanity. With this philosophy, communities were organised and identified as units of varying size and power such as families, clans, villages, and nations (Setumu, 2021). It should be noted that while the concept of Ubuntu has been practiced by many African societies since time immemorial, it was only in the 1990s that it was adapted as an ideology by post-apartheid South Africa, as a vehicle to bring about harmony and cooperation among its many racial and ethnic groups. When Europe colonised Africa, the continent was a vast expanse of open land. The people understood the open country. Unlike colonisers' Eurocentric approaches, African communities understood that resources should be owned, used, and shared by all people. This philosophy and way of life extended to memories that were shared in various forms by individuals, families, communities, and nations, around the fire and at the feasts. In this regard, what is considered "records" in the Western context differs from what is considered "records" in the African context, although definitions by some Western authors are closer to indigenous archives. Prior to colonialism, records in Africa were kept through memories, oral histories, murals, nomenclatures, and rock art paintings. By the end of the 19th century, most indigenous communities had been defeated and had abandoned their conventional practice, embracing the European way of keeping records (Ngoepe & Setumu, 2022). Forced removal of communities by colonial and apartheid governments also played a role in individuals losing their identity and culture. This is also happening in democratic South Africa where mining companies from overseas are forcing communities to relocate. It should be emphasised that some pre-colonial practices have survived and in certain spaces were sustained in secret; hence, we are able to recall the past. Since this subjugation implicitly involved disruption to and attempted destruction of pre-colonial archival modes, it is necessary to conceptualise indigenous archives for the purpose of setting theory and praxis of reconstructing indigenous archives in the postcolonial era.

For a long time in Africa, the archival arena has been dominated by Western discourse, principles, and theories, from the "Dutch Manual" of Muller, Fruin and Fruth, to the work of Jenkinson and later Schellenberg. In the postcolonial era, there has been a recognition that Western epistemology has failed to "embrace indigenous systems of archives, memory, and evidence" (Harris, 1997). Until very recently, archival discourse from countries such as Canada, the United States, and Australia focused on decolonisation, while in southern Africa, the focus is on transformation, decolonisation, and (re)Africanisation in order to reimagine archives that are inclusive or, at least, in the Canadian concept, form part of 'total archives.' However, total archives, just like the Canadian democracy and liberalism, are viewed by Ghaddar (2021) as a tradition rooted in Western imperialism and white supremacy. However, in our context we looked at the concept as framed by the Consultative Group on Canadian Archives as more inclusive, while we acknowledge that inclusivity can be a tall order. It should be noted that in some parts of Africa, archivists are still quite invested in the Western ideologies they were educated in. As such, decolonial work and (re)Africanisation have a long way to go. (Re)Africanisation in this regard is the route to the ability of African people to understand, relate to, and accept their ancestral core (Cannon, 1997).

Reconstructed nations like South Africa are working to develop their national identity. In South Africa, the essence of transformation is covered by Harris (1997; 2000) as he argues that archives are understood as institutions of social memory as they preserve heritage resources and should be conceptualised and integrated within the broader heritage sector. In this regard, he regards archives as promoting a shared heritage identity. Past collecting policies of mainstream institutions in South Africa have skewed the collection of non-public records in such a way that the experiences of a number of communities are poorly documented. South Africa's transition to democracy and transformation

Conceptualisation and recontextualisation of constructs 11

discourse in archives have delivered a refigured archival profession in which black South Africans achieved a representative presence. As observed by Rodrigues (2016), archival participation of certain groups, such as religious and ethnic minority groups, indigenous black communities, immigrant groups, and so on, has been limited in South Africa's archival collections, and therefore the historic picture presented by archival repositories understates the diversity of the nation's actual heritage. This is also the case in Zimbabwe as observed by Bhebhe (2019), who notes that the minority groups are excluded from the national archival system even when oral history projects are undertaken. In the context of a newly formed democracy like South Africa, which is based on equality, there needs to be an effort within the archives and heritage sectors to incorporate all these under-represented voices. In incorporating the indigenous archives, there is a need to focus on discourse of indigenous epistemological and phenomenological richness.

This chapter justifies the need to recall the past through exploring indigenous archives in a postcolonial context by discussing concepts such as oral history, murals, and rock art paintings and their practices as archives in indigenous knowledge systems. As Lemieux (2001) points out, there is no single way to conceptualise a record, just as there are many shades of grey. Rodrigues (2016) also contends that archives vary across different settings and cultural contexts, driven by considerations such as social justice, a focus on common identities and experiences, and a desire to document communities that are historically under-represented. It is hoped that the conceptualisation of indigenous archives in this chapter will add to the ongoing debate and help in the reconstruction of archives that are inclusive, as well as alleviate underrepresentation in the archives. The chapter demonstrates different ways in which African societies created, shared, and preserved records. First, the concepts of archive and record are revisited.

Archives and records revisited

In their chapter on archives and indigenous communities, Faulkhead and Thorpe (2017) acknowledge that indigenous archives do not fit into the dominant worldview of the archival field. What is considered an archive or record by indigenous communities in many African countries and still colonised countries like Canada, Australia, and the United States is different from what is considered an archive or record in the Western canon. According to ISO Standard 15489:2001, the "international" standard for records management, which enshrines at a global level, ideas that emerge from key archival texts of Europe and North America, a record is 'information created, received, and maintained as evidence or information by an organisation or person in pursuance of legal obligations or in the transaction of business.' The National Archives and Records Service of South Africa Act (No. 43 of 1996) similarly defines a record as recorded information, regardless of form or medium, created or received by governmental bodies, while "archives" refer to records in the custody of an archive repository. A closer look at the definitions indicates a greater leaning towards legal organisations or individuals but excludes indigenous memories as a 'record or archive.' As Yeo (2007) would concur, definitions have a bad press as theorists and linguists are not sure of their value. Indeed, definitions can have value within the context in which they are used in particular communities; hence, we propagate that a definition of records or archives be extended to indigenous memories.

The classification of definitions of a record by Yeo (2007) includes those by authors who are shaped by Western archival education and centre their definitions on evidence, authenticity, and contextual provenance, as well as those who see records as information assets for government or business. However, there are also those who see records as impartial, those who prefer to see records evolve to accommodate new types of records, and those that were not considered records. Archives have evolved. Records are used as a narrative of events, actions, communities, and lives. Most of the definitions or viewpoints acknowledge a close connection between records and the activities of individuals, families, communities, or organisations. It should be noted that a record always points to the past, whether the event or activity was recorded a few hours ago or many centuries ago (Yeo, 2007).

A more expansive definition is given by Derrida (1996), who defines an archive as the trace of a process or event inscribed on an internal or external substrate. In this regard, as argued by Harris (1997) the term may include anything recorded as diverse as a tattoo or orality as a record. For example, Van der Merwe (2019) focused on community-based embroidered story cloth projects as a means to give black South African women a voice in the archival process. In this regard, the cloths were used as a record to tell the story. This implies that memories created by individuals, families, or indigenous communities can also be considered a record within the suggestions given.

In this book, the adopted definition is not limited to a public or private institution but also extends to memories of individuals, families, or communities. This human record can bridge time and space to remain meaningful and useful. Archives are a critical component of how societies remember, are held accountable, and generally conduct their affairs. Based on the adopted definition, we will now look at what is considered a memory or a record by the indigenous people of southern Africa. In this regard, we will discuss oral history (using only family praise and nomenclature as examples of preservation of memories in African practice as records), rock art paintings, and murals, termed 'extended archives' by Ngoepe and Mosako (2022), as defined later in the chapter.

Orality

Oral memory has been used in Africa and elsewhere, particularly in Canada and Australia, in 'indigenous knowledge systems into the Western-dominant archival dialogue'. It is not always the case that community archives should be integrated into the national archival system, but where it happens, they should not be subjugated or swallowed. Gilliland (2014) cites the Koorie Heritage Archive in Australia as an example of a community-centric archive that uses orality as archives.

Many archival scholars in southern Africa, including Ngoepe (2019; 2020a; 2022), Bhebhe and Ngoepe (2021a; 2022), Matshotshwane and Ngoepe (2022a; 2022b), and Setumu (2010; 2015), wrote about oral history and how it can be used to fill perceived gaps in mainstream archives, contributing to inclusive archives. Only Ngoepe (2022), Ngoepe and Setumu (2022), and Qwabe (2013) used family praise as a record in their studies. This chapter focuses on two aspects of indigenous archives that use orality to preserve memory: family praise and nomenclature of events, people, and places. We do not focus on the conversion of oral memory to paper or digital format because this has been comprehensively covered in previous studies. According to Harris

(1997), it is common to underestimate the difficulty of converting orality into recorded form.

Oral transmission through memory practices such as family praises or praise poems has been used by Africans to store and transmit valuable information from generation to generation since time immemorial (Ngoepe, 2022). A praise poem is a poem of tribute or gratitude described by Mphande (2008, p. 71) as follows:

> ...Praise poetry is central to any delineation of southern African literature since praising is an important part of the peoples' political and literary expression. The genre of praise poetry called izibongo in Zulu (used in its plural form) is a political art form found in southern African societies like the Nguni- and Sotho-Tswana-speaking peoples. The term refers to the form of poetic expression that defines and names an individual and is characterized by bold imagery expressed in carefully selected language. This type of poetry applies to the personal set of praise names of individuals, comprising cumulative series of praises and epithets bestowed on them by their associates, from childhood onwards, interspersed with narrative passages or comments. These praises, composed and recited by professional bards, often embody concise allusions to historical incidents and memorable achievements or characteristics connected with each family, and may amount to verses of considerable length and excellence. The major function of praise poetry is to conserve and transmit social consciousness, while simultaneously entertaining the audience. Because it deals with happenings in and around the individual being praised, informing the audience of his/her political and social views, praise poetry is documentary, and speakers of many (and similar) southern African languages have retained this cultural expression to aid them in remembering their past.

Through family praises, one can compile a genealogical family tree and trace their ancestral roots. Ngoepe (2020b) indicates that the information in the biography of Ludwick Mamabolo, the 2012 Comrades Marathon champion, was obtained from oral tradition through Benjamin Mamabolo, as well as from family praise, which is also considered a source of information and which proved valuable in providing needed information to trace the ancestral roots of a champion from central Africa to Zimbabwe and then to modern-day South Africa. Lamla (2013) uses family praises as well in his account of King Mthimkhulu of the Hlubi nation when indicating that in King Mthimkhulu's name "umuthi" means "tree" and "omkhulu" means "Great," hence "Mthimkhulu" means "Great Tree." Apparently, he got this name because he had knowledge of kingship medicine and rainmaking on which neighbouring kingdoms such as King Sobhuza I of Swazi nation consulted with him.

Praise poems are composed not only about chiefs, famous warriors, and prominent members of the nobility but also about ordinary people, including women and herdsmen (Mphande, 2008). Individuals and clans have praise poems about them, especially distinguished individuals in societies such as chiefs, the brave, and artists. The histories of the tribal institution of chieftaincy are also expressed in traditional war songs, oral tradition, praise poems, and other cultural forms which distinguish each ethnic and tribal entity from the others. Family praise can be used to trace events and ancestral roots. For example, in the family clan of Ngwepe, also interchangeably Ngoepe (hereby referred to as Ngoepe), family members are able to trace ancestral roots through praise poems to the seventh generation without the aid of government records, even before the surname Ngoepe came into being. In the introductory line of the family praise "Ngoepe 'a Mashokwe' a Tlabo…," which indicates the succession lineage of the identity of who Ngoepe was. It is clear that the surname was adopted during the reign or time of Ngoepe, as his sons adopted his name as surnames, in the late 1700s. Before that, clan names and totems were used. The family praise indicates that Ngoepe was the son of Mashokwe, who was the son of Tlabo. These are Bakone people who, today, fall under the larger Northern Sotho group. If surnames were adopted during the time of Mashokwe, the adopted surname would have been Mashokwe; if during Tlabo's era, it would have been Tlabo. This Ngoepe character is portrayed as a great bull who was deployed by King Matlala to block the cliffs at the Makgabeng mountains, which are on the border of the Matlala and Malebogo nations in Limpopo province of South Africa. Merely reciting the family praise gives the history of the people of Makgabeng their relation to Matlala, and all the other activities they were popular with. Of interest is that the praise even identifies strategic points where Ngoepe and his few family members would hide when the warriors of Mzilikazi passed during the Mfecane. As Qwabe (2013) would attest, traditional praise poets were considered mouths that tell no lies but capture events in a poetic way as they unfolded. Hence, Ngoepe would not hide the line in his family praise that he did hide from Ndebele warriors.

Qwabe (2013, p. 1) also mentions two lines written by Magolwana of Mkhathini Jiyane in reference to King Dingane fleeing when his army was about to be defeated, referring to him as "the restless one; the one who runs away and leaves his army." Ngoepe, Setumu and Ngoepe (2014) report in their historical book 'Bakone ba Makgabeng' that in 1945, Sankobela Ngoepe, a village chief in the Makgabeng area, west of Polokwane in the Limpopo province of South Africa, added lines to his family praise when refusing to buy his own land from the boers. This was a way of creating a record to capture events; in this regard, the refusal to buy his own land. As Setumu (2021) points out, it was ironic that black people were purchasing their own land, which they never sold to whites. Sankobela captured a record through his poetic praise as he relinquished his power as village chief by stating that

Ke ntlatlana, ke hlagetše (I am as old as a worn basket)

Ke seroto serwala dinama ba olela ka nna melora (A basket meant for carrying meat is now used to clear away ashes)

Some of his supporters also refused to purchase their own land. When reciting his family praise, he would refer to himself as the basket that carries meat, but when his subjects were forced to relocate, he had nothing to carry but the remnants (ashes). The praise has a deep meaning and message because it reflects the activities and events of the day. This says a lot about orality in this context, in the form of family praise that has been passed down from generation to generation but has never been documented until now. The creator of such a record in this regard is the chief himself, and it is passed on orally to the receiver (next generation) at a certain point in time. Disposal of such memory is when there is interruption due to death and other factors. Such oral history is not recorded, but rather shared when people are in their natural setting and have a conversation narrating their stories, as opposed to someone recording a story about them. It should be noted that there are families who do not know their origins and family praises due to urbanisation, migration, land dispossession, removal, and other factors.

Setumu (2021) also offers various explanations and interpretations of the surname Moloto, which is the royal family of Bahlaloga in the west of Polokwane, the capital city of the Limpopo province in South Africa. In the family praise, Moloto, as King of Bahlaloga, is credited with saving and protecting his people, as the name indicates. According to Setumu (2021), the praise poem of one of Moletji's kings, Khwinana, indicates that "he is the axe that chopped Dikgale and Mothiba people." This refers to his victory when, after defeating King Dikgale and King Mothiba, he extended his kingdom to the northeast of Polokwane, towards the areas of King Dikgale and King Mothiba. The praise of the Mabotja family demonstrates that the Mabotja people had been the original inhabitants of the Moletji area before King Moloto's people. Mabotja's family praise indicates that Mabotja left Moletji upon Moloto's arrival and later returned.

In Zimbabwe, the Bhebhe clan's relationship with King Mzilikazi is noted in their praises, especially when they say *umaziwa yinkosi* (the one known by the king). This refers to the fact that one of the great medicine men for King Mzilikazi, who was more of a healer for the king, was from the Bhebhe clan. This great medicine man was known as *Tumbale*, hence the Bhebhes found in Zimbabwe are also referred to as *Tumbale* in their clan praises. The historical migration of the Bhebhe people from South Africa can be traced through their clan praises, as the words in their recitations become a mixture of Nguni and Rozwi languages as a result of Mfecane migration during the 1800s. In their clan praise recitations, the Bhebhes of Zimbabwe are also referred to as Mhlongo because they trace their origins to South Africa, where Mhlongo is a very common surname and has a close relationship with the Bhebhe cognomen. As a result, the Bhebhe clan's praises are summarised as *makhedama, Bhebhe, Mhlongo, soyengwase, njomane kamgabhi, dlomo wemdl'ende, wena wase langeni, nzinda, m'zi'mkhulu, maziwayinkosi abanye bengaziwa, mthekele, njomane,* meaning the one known by the king whilst others are not known, and a lot of historical information can be learnt. In other words, these clan praise poetries are the archival repositories of their history, including their origins.

While praise poems are mainly observable for prominent members of society, each clan has its particular praise poem. This means in the southern African context, everyone is included, individually, through the clans and then through the nation. In the Makgabeng area, for example, clans sang long praise poems during important ceremonies and occasions. The Setumu people praise themselves as "Ba maja-a-beela baeng ..." (the ones who when eating also reserve food for visitors), with the Masekwa people being praised as "Ba ga Mmantšana a Botlokwa ..." (showing their origins as Botlokwa). These praise poems are clear identities with which the clans express themselves, just as one has identity documents in Western civilisation. Setumu (2010) emphasises that people's names are praise poems, which are also still a powerful identity marker in Makgabeng and other areas. This is also the case even in other regions such as the KwaZulu-Natal province in South Africa, as well as the Kingdom of Eswatini where people are known through their clan names such as Mapholoba for Ngcobo, Mtungwa for Khumalo, Khabazela for Mkhize, Sibakhulu for Dlamini, Shenge for Buthelezi, Msholozi or Nxamalala for Zuma, Ndosi for Cele and Mvelase for Mthembu, to mention just a few. Mphande (2008) contends that clans are usually named after the founder of the clan.

As praise poems are used to decipher the history of a family, clan, or nation, we consider them a record, given the definition suggested by Derrida (1996). These few examples provided fit the definition of a record. True to the argument by Cook (1992), archival identity has been shifting across four mindsets, that is, juridical legacy, cultural memory, societal engagement, and community archiving. This move is from evidence to memory, to identity, and to community. Nomenclature also suggests an archival move in this direction.

Nomenclature

In many African contexts, memories are preserved in many ways. One such way is the nomenclature of people, events, and activities. In his autoethnography, retired Judge Bernard Ngoepe (2022) talks about the naming practices in some families. This is done according to fixed rules, and it has cultural significance. According to Judge Ngoepe (2022), the practice contributes to the cohesion of families and the retention of family values. This is done among many ethnic groups, albeit with varying permutations and degrees of rigidity. Just as an example, in certain clans such as Ngoepe, the eldest son of a couple would be named after the child's paternal grandfather, irrespective of its gender. If the gender is different from the grandfather's, the name would be corrupted by taking the closest corresponding name. For example, if a child is a girl named after the grandfather, who is Solomon, such a child might be named Salmina or Albertina for Albert (Ngoepe, 2022). The second child is named after its maternal grandfather, the third after its paternal grandmother, and the fourth after its maternal grandmother, with the subsequent ones named after the aunt (father's sister) and the uncle (mother's brother). The names of aunts and uncles are used in the order of their seniority. Ngoepe (2022) emphasises that naming without regard for gender serves two purposes: it does not disrupt the pattern of naming, which remains predictable (just as information is stored in order, for example, through a classification system), and no one is excluded because of gender non-correspondence. This naming practice can be used by a person to trace their genealogy. It is one way of keeping family trees and genealogical research can be deciphered based on the naming convention if one is able to understand and interpret it.

The naming of places, events, or activities is another method of keeping a record through nomenclature. Setumu (2021, p. 30) provides examples of the naming of the Mogalakwena River (crocodile) as follows:

> When the Bakwena people flew from the Nguni attacks, they came across a big river which they were unable to cross — they literally believed that the river refused their crossing. One leader suggested that they should give the river a name and that it would allow them to cross. Many names were suggested, and they eventually settled for the name "Mogana," which means "the refuser", as it refused the Dikwena to cross. The name later evolved into "Moganakwena" (refusing Dikwena to cross), which later became "Mogalakwena," as the river is known today. One of the servants of the king from the main royal house, Maleka (whose name means the one who tries because

of this event), is linked to the Sesotho proverb that says "*go leka noka ga se go wela*", literally meaning to try to cross is not to fall in the river, constructed a crossing equipment using the river reeds and some branches. The equipment is called 'lehlaloga' from where the name 'Batlhaloga' would evolve. To this day, these people are known as Batlhaloga.

The other example provided by Setumu (2021) is the name of the school 'Seripa' and the name of the village 'Tibu,' near the small town of Senwabarwana (Bochum). The school and the village were named in honour of the recalcitrant Batlhaloga warrior regent, Seripa. Seripa was once a regent and refused to hand over power to the heir, Seshego. To solve the impasse between Seripa and Seshego, the royal elders called a huge gathering and brought a watermelon. They agreed to break the watermelon in half; one half would represent Seripa and the other half would represent Seshego. The bet was that the half that contained the tibu (the big juicy heart of the melon) would be the winner and thereby become the ruler. After breaking the watermelon, the lot (tibu) fell on Seripa, making him the winner. When he was denied ruling after winning the toss, Seripa broke away from Batlhaloga and took his followers with him. He is purported to have said: "Mpheng seripa sa ka (give me my portion/half)." This is how he got the name Seripa (portion). He later bought the land that was named gaTibu, and the high school that was built there was named Seripa.

Mutonhori (2014, p. 51) argues that

> among the Ndebele, as is the case with most cultures in Africa, the concept of naming actually mirrors the Ndebele people and their environment, which is, but not limited to, their experiences, fears, and worldviews. In addition to that, naming among the Ndebele is like a statement, and that statement should be addressing a particular subject.

Therefore, names given to children such as Sibangilizwe (fighting for the country), Sifelani (what are we dying for) and uMumowezwe (the state of the country) were more popular during the liberation struggle in Zimbabwe. Other prevalent names during this period were Butholezwe (army of the nation), Mayihlome (let's take up

Conceptualisation and recontextualisation of constructs 21

arms), Melimpi (stand up for war), Thulilwempi (the dust of war), Dumolwempi (the ubiquity of war), Hlaselani (you should attack), and Qoqanani (organise yourselves) (Mutonhori 2014, p. 52). In other words, these names play a major role in documenting the liberation struggle against colonialism.

Rock art paintings

Another form of recording in the African context is rock art paintings. Many authors wrote about this topic, especially from the archaeological perspective. Rock art paintings have been used by African ancestors to preserve information and communicate messages to the next generations. As Setumu (2015, p. 35) would attest, African ancestors also left messages and stories in the form of symbols etched on the rocks. Such information on the rocks has not been considered records by Western archival standards. For the purpose of this chapter, we used the rock art paintings of the Khoisan and Bantu-speaking people in the mountains of Makgabeng in the Limpopo province of South Africa as examples (See Figure 1.1 and Figure 1.2).

Figure 1.1 Rock art paintings by the San people.

22 *Conceptualisation and recontextualisation of constructs*

Figure 1.2 Rock art paintings by the Bantu-speaking people.

The Makgabeng plateau covers an area of 225 square kilometres and lies to the southwest of Blouberg mountain, with an elevation of 1159 m. It is one of four distinct rock art areas of the central Limpopo Basin, the others being Soutpansberg, the Limpopo/Shashe confluence and north-eastern Venda. One of the outstanding features of Makgabeng is the Khoisan and Bantu-speaking rock art paintings in the mountains. In Zimbabwe, most, if not all, of the rock art paintings were mainly done by the Khoisan people, and this phenomenon is very noticeable at Matopo National Park. The fine paintings are evidence of traces of the earliest human occupation in the area. Of the utmost importance is that these rock art paintings have withstood the test of time. The rock art in Figure 1.2 is thought to have been painted around early 1900 by the local Bantu people along the same spot (see Figure 1.1) as those painted many moons ago by the Khoisan people. Each of the paintings has meaning. The painting by Bantu-speaking people reflects events after the Malebogo boer war that took place in 1894. Apparently, King Seketa Lebogo of the Bahananwa dynasty refused to have his territory demarcated in 1888 by the Boer Republic. He also refused to have his huts recorded for tax purposes in 1891. As a result, General Piet Joubert of the Boer Republic besieged his fortress from the first half of June to the end of July 1894. The Bahananwa put up a very brave fight but were defeated. King Lebogo was tried and jailed in Pretoria as a prisoner of war. Some of his followers were jailed with him. Upon release, when they got back home, they painted the rock art, revealing their emotions as well as what they saw when they were in Pretoria, that is, railways with a train on tracks and boers riding on horses, as reflected in the paintings.

These world-class rock art paintings have been on the radar of the South African Heritage Resource Agency for national declaration, with the ultimate goal of a possible international declaration of the sites by the United Nations Educational, Scientific and Cultural Organization (Setumu, 2010). In an interview with Fortune Mabeba, Makgabeng Farm Lodge owner in Bochum (South Africa) on 31 July 2015, it was revealed that the painting traditions of farmers, herders, and hunter-gatherers co-occur differently. About half the sites contain either Northern Sotho or San paintings, while the other half are a combination of two or even three of the traditions. This indicates that there was almost certainly some cultural interaction between the three groups, that is, Northern Sotho with finger paintings, Khoekhoe herder with finger paintings and San hunter-gatherer with fine-line paintings. Today, the area is occupied by the Northern Sotho group.

Murals

The concept of murals as records can also be used to decolonise the definition of archives. During the pre-colonial era in South Africa, such practice was first explored by the San society through rock and cave paintings. In the context of this study, murals are discussed as a modern extension of rock art. As such, murals can be used to decolonise archives while rock art can be used to (re) Africanise archives. Ngoepe and Mosako (2022) discuss murals as a type of record. Ngoepe and Mosako (2022) consider murals as extended archives, bringing archives to the people. The authors define "extended archives" as archival groups depicted as murals on the walls, while the original archives displayed are in an archive repository. Murals like the ones depicted in Figure 1.3 are from the Letlamoreng Dam precinct in Mafikeng, South Africa's North

24 *Conceptualisation and recontextualisation of constructs*

Figure 1.3 Mural of Barolong kings.

West province, which is based on archival images displayed. The archive images displayed at the Letlamoreng Dam depict a line-up of the Barolong, an ethnic group in Mahikeng, as well as iconic figures who played critical leadership roles in Mahikeng, such as Sol Plaatjie, the African National Congress's first secretary general (1912–1915). The original photographs are kept at the North West Provincial Archives Repository in Mahikeng, hence Ngoepe and Mosako (2022) label them 'extended archives.' Murals of this type can be permanent or temporary, internal (inside a building) or external (on the walls), and they can be large or small in scale. Internal murals commemorating struggle icons who interacted with the Alexandra Township during the apartheid years can be found in Alexandra Township inside Alex Mall (GPS Coordinates: 26.1054°S, 28.1216°E) (Ngoepe and Mosako 2022).

Conceptualisation and recontextualisation of constructs 25

Figure 1.4.1 Mural of mayors of the City of eThekwini.

Another example of large external mural depiction can be found at the KARA Heritage Institute (GPS Coordinates: 25°44′47″S 28°10′53″E / 25.74639°S 28.18139°E) in Pretoria (South Africa), as well as the one for mayors of the City of eThekwini since 1995 (see Figure 1.4.1) as one enters Durban from Pietermaritzburg via the N3 road. Previously, on the same site, there was a mural of kings who ruled the Zulu nation from King Shaka (1818–1828) to King Misuzulu (2022–) (see Figure 1.4.2). Passers-by, as reflected in the picture, stop and view the mural.

In Zimbabwe, one can find contemporary murals like the one depicted in Figure 1.5. The muralist, Leeroy Spinx Brittain, also known as Bow, addressed the problem of tribalism in Zimbabwe by evoking respectable historical figures such as the past Ndebele King Lobengula and the Shona spirit medium Mbuya Nehanda, who was recently memorialised by the current government by erecting a statue of her in Harare Central Business District. Bow is quoted in Dube (2022) as saying, "In Matabeleland, people give so much respect and honour to King Lobengula, and in Mashonaland, it is

Figure 1.4.2 Mural of the kings who ruled the Zulu nation from 1818 to present.

Mbuya Nehanda, and what the piece means is that a Shona and a Ndebele can love each other." Unfortunately, rather than uniting the people as the muralist hoped, the mural bred tribalism and was eventually erased by the Bulawayo Municipal City Council.

Figure 1.5 Mural of late King Lobengula of the Ndebele nation in Zimbabwe.

Interestingly, the day after the mural was erased, the people of Bulawayo awoke to another mural protesting the Gukurahundi massacres painted on the same wall. The anonymous muralist in this case painted the words "Gukurahundi, we will not forget." The graffiti text was written in black with a splash of red paint to imply bloodshed (Dube, 2022).

Murals are not unique to Africa. It should be noted that other nations outside Africa also use murals as records. For example, the picture in Figure 1.6 was captured in the Anthropology Museum in Mexico City. The mural recreates the daily activities in the village in the ancient era. It can be seen how man, from very early times, chose the most favourable places for his development. He settled near water sources where he fished and hunted using baskets, nets, and spears. He cultivated the nearby lands preparing them by clearing or burning, for which he used axes and planting sticks; and in the nearby forests, he collected various plants.

28 *Conceptualisation and recontextualisation of constructs*

Figure 1.6 Mural of the daily activities of an ancient village in Mexico.

In South Africa, such archives can be created at a variety of sites. Ordinary people can identify with such mural products because they see them every day and would eventually visit archive repositories to access the actual archive. Murals can be used to bring archives to the people in this way. Portraying murals as extended archives provides a one-of-a-kind platform for bringing archives to the people and raising public awareness of archive repositories. It also aids in the reconstruction of records that are no longer in existence or are in an archive repository, just like the one from Mexico City depicted in Figure 1.6. This, in turn, proves the intersection of archives and other fields such as history, anthropology, and archaeology. According to Gilliland (2014), many fields perceive themselves as inextricably linked to information, memory, and evidence in some form or another, although the profession of the record is archival science and records management.

As an affirmation of the extended archives practice, Kastanakis and Voyer (2014) argue that any cultural product can be marketed and promoted in any space, irrespective of whether the space is an African region or a non-African region, and/or a Western region or a non-Western region. The benefit of such versatility in the promotion and marketing of cultural products lies in the undertaking of a sociological phenomenon such as cross-cultural understanding and historical teaching using public spaces. The depiction of archives as murals may stimulate a positive interest in the public in archival holdings. In South Africa and other African countries, such an interest can be achieved by means of commissioning projects to paint murals on local geographic walls. One of the muralists in Zimbabwe, popularly known as Bow, suggested "I wish the city council could give us a platform and give us walls in the high-density suburbs so that we can communicate and tell our stories" (Dube, 2022, p. 13).

Halls of honour, like murals, can be used to decolonise archives. A hall of honour can be a room, building, or wall with memorabilia set aside to honour outstanding individuals in any profession, locality, nation, or the like. The Comrades Marathon Hall of Honour is one such example, located along the Comrades route at a point where the road overlooks the Valley of a Thousand Hills. Runners who completed the Comrades Marathon can mount their numbers on a plaque on this wall, as shown in Figure 1.7.

According to the Comrades Marathon Association, the wall was built several years ago to serve as a permanent landmark to commemorate the accomplishments of Comrades Marathon runners who completed the epic journey between Pietermaritzburg and Durban. The wall is made of attractive interlocking blocks, similar to those used for retaining walls. Runners who complete the Comrades Marathon successfully can purchase their own blocks in perpetuity. These are mounted on an attractive plaque that records the runner's name, race number, and status, which can be updated in later years. Besides providing historical information on runners, tourists often stop at this landmark.

Intersection of indigenous archives with technology

Oral and physical instantiations of 'the record' can also intersect with the digital, which has reshaped understandings of records and archives in a way that indigenous knowledge practices have not yet

30 *Conceptualisation and recontextualisation of constructs*

Figure 1.7 The Comrades Marathon Hall of Honour.

been allowed to do. Many studies mention technology as a tool that can be used to preserve indigenous knowledge by converting it from one medium to another, such as oral to paper or digital. However, in this section, we concentrate on the opportunities

Conceptualisation and recontextualisation of constructs 31

provided by technologies. We believe that in the digital era, technologies are opening up archives to people like never before, allowing local, national, and global audiences to gain historical information. The advantages of incorporating digital technology into what we call indigenous archives are numerous, and such benefits cannot be overlooked. As a result, any field of study that does not embrace digital technologies will become obsolete in the end. Archival science, like indigenous knowledge systems, is not an exception. Technology, through virtual exhibitions, can be used to bring indigenous archives to digital natives. Murals, extended archives, oral records, nomenclature, and rock art paintings, as shown and discussed above, provide such an opportunity. In this regard, digital technology can be used to raise awareness of indigenous archives by linking the depicted murals and rock art paintings to the Google Maps application. Syms (2019) best summarises these Google interconnection apps as follows:

- **Cities Talking**: With Cities Talking, users can listen to a guided tour narrated by locals through artificial intelligence software. The app offers GPS-enabled maps, a guidebook, and descriptions that can be read while the audio plays. The app also displays nearby places of interest, such as heritage sites and local murals.
- **GPSmyCity**: Users can create their own self-guided walking tours or tour routes on the map. Like a GPS, this app gives turn-by-turn walking directions, which can be shared on social media. The fact that GPSmyCity works offline may be an added advantage for some end-users, as it removes the risk of international roaming charges.
- **Geotourist**: It simply finds the user's location and displays nearby attractions and landmarks. One needs to select the desired destination and an audio, guided tour created by other app users will be played. That means anyone with the app can also create their own audio, tag it, and share it on social media or within the Geotourist app for others to access.
- **Field Trip**: For users interested in off-the-beaten-path landmarks, there is Field Trip (by Google). The app notifies users when an interesting landmark is nearby, including historic places, food, drink, stores, products, and even music events and local murals.

They can view photos, read descriptions, and learn about the attractions before venturing inside.
- History **Pin**: While not exactly an app, this browser-based programme is perfect for history buffs. History Pin shows your current location as it once looked in the past. When you toggle your phone's camera over your current location, a series of historic photos appear. History Pin also offers historic guided tours so you can tour a city in the context of the past. Tour narrations are sourced both by users and by verified historical institutions.

Through these apps, the general public can have thrilling archival engagements and informative experiences during and after the onsite or virtual tour, as well as through smart tourism. Ödemiş (2022) describes smart tourism as the type of tourism that requires the integration of many factors and components such as information technology infrastructure services, well-trained human resources, effective promotion and marketing practices, cooperation between stakeholders and environmental awareness. Just like educational programmes, as Mukwevho (2018) argues, extended archives can serve as an interactive tool for public engagement and can promote inclusive public participation. Digital tourism is supported by digital technology that can link Google apps to murals. Apart from the benefit that arises from using murals as a vehicle to populate archives in the public space, more can be done to encourage people to gain an interest in using and understanding archives. Furthermore, as Ngoepe (2022) suggests, archivists can investigate the possibility of using artificial intelligence technologies to acquire and capture oral memory, as well as establish links between oral histories and recordings over time. This can be done taking into consideration that the moment oral sources are captured by whatever gadget or means, they cease to be oral. Indigenous archives have the potential to show opportunities for archives in 'ancestral tourism.' This might encourage the African diaspora to visit archives as tourists in order to obtain family history information from archives.

Through the applications, more benefits can be explored where the all-pervading phenomenon of taking archives to the multitudes through murals is comprehended. Positively, such a multitude can connect with other multitudes throughout the world through

Conceptualisation and recontextualisation of constructs 33

digital applications and platforms such as Google Connect and the technological medium of the digital age (Szekely, 2017). These current digital application perspectives may also expand an earlier argument by Cartiere and Willis (2008) on localised public displays and mural images, which are often site specific.

In South Africa, there are orality projects through technology that are already underway. For example, the importance of orality is recognised through the conception of the Ancestral Voices project, which takes the reader back to pre-colonial times. The project contains the earliest recorded statements by speakers of now official indigenous languages in South Africa on the history, indigenous knowledge systems, and every aspect of the traditional cultural practices of their people, as recorded by authors who were also mother-tongue speakers of the language concerned, many after interviewing the then elderly, which, in many instances, takes us back to pre-colonial times.[1]

Furthermore, there are a number of rock art painting projects, such as the African Rock Art Digital Archive. According to its website, the goal of the Ringing Rocks Digital Laboratory and The African Rock Art Digital Archive (SARADA) is to digitise rock art collections on the African continent, make them available in an easily searchable database, and in so doing, convey the importance of protecting and preserving the continent's rich archaeological heritage and facilitating ongoing research and interest in its fascinating past.[2]

Conclusion

In this chapter, the concepts of orality (looking only at family praises and nomenclature as records), rock art paintings, and murals were used to conceptualise indigenous archives as archival. Although Western constructs define a 'record' differently, the identified types of information sources are obscured from Western archival view but are considered records from an African perspective. As a result, Western canons and the international standards shaped by them, as well as African archival legislation that perpetuates Eurocentric notions of the record and considers a record to exist in four media (paper, electronic, microfilm, and audio-visual format), must be extended to these identified indigenous archives. A wider application of the definition of a record is desired. In this way, archival thought will embrace multiple modes of knowing and archiving, as well as multiple types of archival records, including indigenous archives, culminating in the archival multiverse identified by Gilliland (2014). Alternative archives that were previously unimaginable are being created by these types of archives (McKemmish, Faulkhead & Russell, 2011). Since there is no organic African model for indigenous archives in the current literature, the suggestions in this chapter can be used as a foundation for archival theorists on the continent to use these cultural roots and reimagine a way of doing things that does not begin with the Eurocentric. This should be done with caution because, according to Bhebhe and Ngoepe (2021b), there is elitism even in critical emancipatory movements because the memories that are often preserved are those of the people in positions of power. The types of archives discussed in this chapter, such as orality (praise poems and nomenclature), murals, rock art paintings, and walls of honour, demonstrate the potential for archives in 'ancestral tourism.' This may encourage local and international visitors to visit these areas as tourists to gather information. While gathering data for this chapter, we observed a number of people viewing murals, rock art paintings, and the Wall of Fame.

The description of indigenous memories in this chapter fits the concept of archives and aligns to the conceptualisation by Harris (2000) that an archive is a construction of the process and the event. It matters to include these indigenous archives in mainstream archival debates because Africa's knowledge system should also contribute to the global system, thereby contributing to solving grand societal problems, as well as reconstructing the past of previously marginalised communities and nations. We hope this chapter will spark debate on the definition of an archive to extend to orality, murals, rock art paintings, and extended archives. This way, a definition of archives in the African context, which does not fit the Western epistemology of records, would be covered. We believe that if these types of records were included in the definition of archives in legislation, it may offer an opportunity not to be missed to Africanise and decolonise archives. Counter archives are emerging in southern Africa to bridge the gap created by colonialism and apartheid and perpetuated by democratic governments. Indigenous archives may also be part of these archives.

Notes

1 More information on Ancestral Voices which is considered the largest heritage and indigenous language preservation project undertaken in South Africa, is accessible via the link www.saheritagepublishers.co.za
2 See the link sarada.co.za for the digitised rock art paintings in Africa.

References

Bhebhe, S. (2019). *Memorialising minority groups in post-independence Zimbabwe and South Africa: a critical analysis of oral history programme*. PhD thesis, Pretoria: University of South Africa.
Bhebhe, S. and Ngoepe, M. (2021a). A forgotten past is the past that is yet to be: evaluation of oral history programme of the Oral History Association of South Africa. *ESARBICA Journal*, 40: 60–78. https://dx.doi.org/10.4314/esarjo.v40i1.5
Bhebhe, S. and Ngoepe, M. (2021b). Elitism in critical emancipatory paradigm: national archival oral history collection in Zimbabwe and South Africa. *Archival Science*, 21: 155–172.
Bhebhe, S. and Ngoepe, M. (2022). Building counter-archives: oral history programmes of the Sinomlando Centre and Memory Work in Africa and the South African History Archive. *Information Development*, 38(2): 257–267.
Buenavista, D.P., Wynne-Jones, S. and McDonald, M. (2018). Asian indigeneity, indigenous knowledge systems, and challenges of the 2030 Agenda. *East Asian Community Rev*, 2018(1): 221–240.
Cannon, J.A. (1997). Re-Africanization: the last alternative for Black America. *Phylon* (1960), 38(2): p. 203–210. https://doi.org/10.2307/274683
Cartiere, C. and Shirley Willis, S. (Eds.). (2008). *The practice of public art*. London: Routledge.
Cook, T. (1992). Easier to byte, harder to chew: the second generation of electronic records archives. *Archivaria*, 33: 202–216.
Derrida, J. (1996). *Archive fever: a Freudian impression*. Chicago: University of Chicago Press.
Dube, S. (2022). Erased mural brews tribal storm. *The Standard Newspaper*, January 30.
Faulkhead, S. and Thorpe, K. (2017). Dedication: archives and indigenous communities. In A.J. Gilliland, S. McKemmish and A.J. Lau. *Research in Archival Multiverse*, Monash University: Clayton, 2–15.
Ghaddar, J.J. (2021). Total archives for land, law and sovereignty in settler Canada. *Archival Science*, 21: 59–82.

Gilliland, A.J. (2014). *Conceptualizing 21st century archives*. Chicago: Society of South American Archivists.
Harris, V. (1997). *Exploring archives: an introduction to archival ideas and practice in South Africa*. 1st ed. Pretoria: National Archives of South Africa.
Harris, V. (2000). *Exploring archives: an introduction to archival ideas and practice in South Africa*. 2nd ed. Pretoria: National Archives of South Africa.
Kastanakis, M.N. and Voyer, B.G. (2014). The effect of culture on perception. *Journal of Archival Organization*, 67(4): 425–433.
Lamla, C.M. (2013). The descendants of Mthimkhulu I. In C. Landman (Ed.), *Oral history: representing the hidden, the untold and the veiled*, Pretoria: University of South Africa, 19–34.
Lemieux, L. (2001). Let the ghosts speak: an empirical exploration of the nature of the record. *Archivaria*, 51: 82.
Matshotshwane, J. and Ngoepe, M. (2022a). Transcending invisible lanes through inclusion of athletics memories in archival systems in South Africa. *HTS Teologiese Studies/Theological Studies*, 78 (3), 10.
Matshotshwane, J. and Ngoepe, M. (2022b). Golden bulb covered with a dark cloth: memories of undocumented athletes in South Africa. *ESARBICA Journal*, 41: 1–17.
McKemmish, S., Faulkhead, S. and Russell, L. (2011). Distrust in the archive: reconciling records. *Archival Science*, 11: 211–239.
Mphande, L. (2008). Heroic and praise poetry in South Africa. In F.A., Irele and S., Gikandi (Eds.). *The Cambridge history of African and Caribbean literature*, Cambridge: Cambridge University Press, 71–97. https://doi.org/10.1017/CHOL9780521832755.006
Mukwevho, J. (2018). Educational programs as an interactive tool for public engagement by public archives repositories in South Africa. *Archives & Manuscript*, 46(3): 302–29.
Mutonhori, T. (2014). The philosophy of naming among the Ndebele of Zimbabwe. A study of the naming system before and after independence, 1970-1982. *International Journal of Humanities and Social Science* 3(3): 51–54.
Ngoepe, B.M. (2022). *Rich pickings out of the past*. Claremont: Juta and Company.
Ngoepe, M. (2019). Archives without archives: a window of opportunity to build inclusive archive in South Africa. *Journal of the South African Society of Archivists*, 52: 149–166.
Ngoepe, M. (2020a). Whose truth is true? The use of archival principles to authenticate oral history. In P. Ngulube (Ed.). *Handbook of research on connecting research methods for information science*, Hershey: IGI Global, 307–319.

Ngoepe, M. (2020b). *Stir the dust: memoirs of a Comrades champion, Ludwick Mamabolo*. Polokwane: Mak Herp.
Ngoepe, M. (2022). Neither prelegal nor nonlegal: oral memory in troubled times. *HTS Teologiese Studies/Theological Studies*, 78(3): 6.
Ngoepe, M. and Mosako, R.D. (2022). Walls have ears and eyes: taking 'extended archives' to the people through murals. *Journal of Archival Organization*, volume ahead of print.
Ngoepe, M. and Setumu, T. (2022). *Setlaole our home: our heritage, history, and culture*. MARKHERP: Polokwane.
Ngoepe, M., Setumu, T. and Ngoepe, S. (2014). *Bakone ba Makgabeng*. Early Dawn Senwabarwana: Traditional Council.
Ödemiş, M. (2022). Smart tourism destinations: a literature review on applications in Turkey's touristic destinations. In N. Gustavo, J. Pronto, L. Carvalho and M. Belo (Eds.), *Optimizing digital solutions for hyper-personalization in tourism and hospitality*, Hershey: IGI Global, 131–153. doi:10.4018/978-1-7998-8306-7.ch007
Qwabe, T. (2013). Daring to challenge the mightiest: voices and acts of bravery found in the oral history of the Zulu people. In C. Landman (Ed.). *Oral History: Heritage and Identity*, 1–6. Pretoria: Department of Arts and Culture.
Rodrigues, A. (2016). Introducing an archival collecting model for the records created by South African Portuguese community organisations. *Archives and Manuscripts*, 44(3): 141–154. 10.1080/01576895.2016.1258582
Setumu, T. (2010). *Communal identity creation among the Makgabeng rural people in Limpopo Province*. PhD Thesis, University of Limpopo, Turfloop.
Setumu, T. (2011). *Hisstory is history: rural village future through the eyes of a rural village boy*. Pretoria: Unisa Press.
Setumu, T. (2015). Inclusion of rural communities in national archival and records system: a case study of Blouberg-Makgabeng-Senwabarwana area. *Journal of South African Society of Archivists*, 48: 34–44.
Setumu, T. (2016). *Africa in the Arts (visual, performance, digital, music): a case study of Blouberg-Makgabeng-Senwabarwana (BMS) Festivals Project*. Paper presented at the UNISA School of Arts Triennial Conference: Exploring the African continent through the Arts: re-mapping, re-thinking, re-imagining Africa. 14–15 September, Pretoria.
Setumu, T. (2021). *Moletji: history of Batlhaloga of Moloto Kingdom*. Polokwane: Mak Herp.
Syms, S. (2019). 10 Apps that'll help you tour a new city: Touring cities with headphones is a fun way to see a city at your own pace. Available at: www.wheretraveler.com/advice/10-apps-thatll-help-you-tour-new-city (Accessed 16 October 2019).

Szekely, I. (2017). Do archives have a future in the digital age? *Journal of Contemporary Archival Studies*, 4. Available at: http://elischolar.library. yale.edu/jcas/vol4/iss2/1 (Accessed 10 October 2021).

Van der Merwe, R. (2019). From a silent past to a spoken future: black women's voices in the archival process. *Archives and Records*, 40(3): 239–258. doi:10.1080/23257962.2017.1388224

Yeo, G. (2007). Concepts of record (1): evidence, information, and persistent representations. *The American Archivist*, 70(Fall/Winter): 315–343.

2 Decolonisation or (re)Africanisation of archives?

Introduction

Given what is considered archives in Chapter One, this chapter examines how colonial governments viewed Africans and their traditions in terms of archiving. The archives left by the colonialists are still steeped in colonial society's history, and indigenous people are only mentioned in passing. An example of this can be found in a photograph in the Cape Town Archives Repository, where the metadata identifies white soldiers by name while an African is identified as an unidentified black soldier (Ngoepe, 2009). According to Ngoepe (2019, p. 159), "archives are supposed to reflect the society in which people live." However, as Callinicos and Odendaal (1996, p. 34) observed in South Africa, at the dawn of democracy, archives revealed the historical biases of colonialism and apartheid. Apartheid grossly distorted the acquisition of and access to records. Indeed, archives were part of a larger system that negated the experiences of black South Africans. For example, in a letter to the editor of the *Sowetan* newspaper, for example, Ngoepe (2009) laments the continued eroding of black people's memory by removing their names from recordings, thereby perpetuating the apartheid style of marginalisation of blacks. This was in response to an article that failed to identify Mbuyiswa Makhuba,[1] but that merely referred to him as just a fellow student of Hector Pietersen.

In essence, the African story was largely neglected unless it had incidental or circumstantial relevance to the colonial occupation of the country. The traditional way of archiving that was mentioned in Chapter One has been forced to the margins. Archival methodology mainly replicates the archival practices of colonisation, imperialism, and, to some extent, apartheid. Therefore, this led to the archival system that silenced African voices. This calls for African archivists to identify ways of decolonising and (re) Africanising archives. It is hoped that the decolonisation and (re) Africanisation of archives will help in the unmuting of the African voices that have been muted for so long. It should, however, be noted that archives, as currently understood, by their nature, are the products of Western or Eurocentric epistemologies, which do not cater to African epistemology. Africa's rich cultural and intellectual traditions were systematically denied during colonisation, hence their absence from the archives, and they did not get enough opportunity to grow, hence they are still considered primitive (Ngoepe, 2022). Therefore, the ways of knowing for the African people automatically are neglected in the Eurocentric archival setup, which was left by the colonialists. In this chapter, decolonisation is linked to Afrocentrism, as we are trying to restore hidden and veiled African memories as archives. Furthermore, the chapter looks into the post-colonial governments, how they view African traditions, what the differences, if any, were, and how they decolonised archives. This helps to show if there is a move towards decolonisation of archives or whether things still resemble the past, as argued by Ketelaar (1992, p. 5) that "what is left after the revolution often resembles the past."

Decolonisation defined

Decolonisation can be defined in different ways, and the scholarship is replete with many different definitions. Bak (2021, p. 423) defines decolonisation as "the process of undoing the harms of colonialism." In locating archives within the structures of colonialism, Bak (2021, p. 424) argues that in the case of Canada, "archives perpetuate legal fictions such as *terra nullius* (or nobody's land, a key justification for Canadian settlement of Indigenous lands) and contribute to the literal overwriting of Indigenous legal and political systems by European[s]...." Therefore, according to Jackson (2020, p. 14), decolonisation is "about disputing, disrupting, and dispensing with the specious assumption that European (i.e., white) and masculinist epistemologies – or regimes of knowledge and modes of reasoning – stand in for universal, objective 'truths'." In applying this definition to archival science, we propose that Eurocentric archival practices can be and must be contested, disrupted, and, to some extent, forced to the margins, so that Afrocentric archivism, which speaks to African knowledge, can be accommodated in the archive's epistemic centre. Hendrickson (2017, p. 321) contends that if the colonial archive is not decolonised, there is a risk that the post-colonial archive will just resemble the old by stating that "this is a postcolonial problem that, without the work of decolonizing the archives, will reproduce new forms of archival regulation by the very states whose peoples were once victims of colonial apparatuses." Hence, Matshotshwane and Ngoepe (2022) argue that as long as archival holdings reflect only colonial archives, the country is still colonised. This is also supported in the conclusion of "The Archival Colour Line" by Linebaugh and Lowry, using a quote from Ghaddar (2021, p. 296), and averring that "among many other abuses that call for redress, we will not have reached a time of true post-coloniality until what was taken has been returned." However, some scholars, such as Carruthers (2019, p. xx), are sceptical of decolonisation because they assume that it is not neutral and "neither has the term's connection to heritage and preservation enjoyed a value-free existence." If not handled properly, it can easily degenerate into populism; it is also sometimes used to serve authoritarian regimes' selfish interests in cementing their grip on power by manipulating public memory.

Africanisation defined

Letsekha (2013, p. 5) defines this post-colonial discourse as a "renewed focus on Africa and entails salvaging what has been stripped from the continent." Africa has been stripped of its dignity through the bastardisation of its knowledge systems by the Western world. The African continent has been qualified by some as the "most humiliated, most dehumanised continent in the world" whose past is "a tale of dispossession and impoverishment" (Osundare, 1998, p. 231). Africanisation, therefore, is a clarion call for the restoration of those knowledge systems, including the African ritual archives as described by Falola (2017). Ramose (1998) argues that

42 Decolonisation or (re)Africanisation of archives?

Africanisation holds that different foundations exist for the construction of pyramids of knowledge. It disclaims the view that any pyramid is by its very nature eminently superior to all others. It is a serious quest for a radical and veritable change of paradigm so that the African may enter into genuine and critical dialogical encounter with other pyramids of knowledge. Africanisation is a conscious and deliberate assertion of nothing more than the right to be African.

Ramose's (1998) argument speaks to the views of the authors of this book because they believe that archival systems should not only be based on Eurocentric epistemology but also on African ways of knowing.

African archiving before the great invasion by the imperialists

As argued in Chapter One, the term "archive" tends to be Eurocentric, with an etymology, intellectual history, and set of foundational concepts that are traced to Western civilisations and traditions. There is no part of this origin story that admits black people and reflects the assumption "that an indigenous person was a savage pagan with no history or culture to transmit" (Seroto, 2011, p. 78), as echoed by Hegel (1956, p. 8), who avers that

> at this point we leave Africa, not even to mention it again. For it is no historical part of the world; it has no movement or development to exhibit. What we properly understand by African is the unhistorical, undeveloped spirits...

Similarly, Trevor-Roper's (1967) most famous anti-African hard-hitting statement is that

> it is fashionable to speak today as if European history were devalued: as if historians in the past have paid too much attention to it, and as if, nowadays, we should pay less. Undergraduates, seduced as always by the changing breath of journalistic fashion, demand that they be taught the history of black Africa. Perhaps, in the future, there will be Africa history to teach. But at present there is none, or very little: there is only history of Europeans in Africa which fit subjects of

proper history. The rest is darkness and darkness is not the subject matter of history. All that happens in Africa before the European contact was mere unrewarding gyrations of barbarous tribes in picturesque.

The myth of an ahistorical Africa is connected with the myth of African illiteracy. One of the eminent English writers by the name Newton is renowned for having said history begins when man takes to writing, the implication of which is that oral communities did not have history to talk about (Davidson, 1964, p. 18). It should be noted, however, that illiteracy as defined from a Western point of view is contextual, as Africans had their own way of writing and communicating messages and information to current and future generations, as well as, to some extent, past generations through spirits, murals, rock art paintings, and oral histories.

However, when archiving is defined as the preservation of history, which includes the keeping of memory, it can be safely stated that archiving existed prior to the invasion of Africa by marauding colonialists. Even though its dictates were very different from Eurocentric archiving principles, Africa had its own ways of preserving its history. Oral traditions, as well as other methods discussed in Chapter One, such as nomenclature, family praises, murals, and rock art paintings, were used to preserve their cultures, histories, and indigenous knowledge systems. Heissig and Schott (1998, p. 26) elaborate on the significance of such African ways of knowing when they state that

> oral traditions, transmitted in the form of tales, myths and legends, fairytales, songs, especially epic songs and poems, proverbs, riddles, and other genres, form an important treasury of many people's cultural heritage even today. Among ethnic groups without a written tradition, almost all knowledge is conveyed orally from one generation to the next, but oral traditions play an important role also among people possessing written texts.

This is the significance of the African oral archive, as seen by Heissig and Schott (1998) as a living museum, conserved and transmitted from one person to another over time. According to Bhebhe (2018, p. 1–2):

African societies, the Ndebele society included, are replete with different forms of traditional literature, which were not only used as pastime as some may claim but were used in raising children to be responsible adults. Most, if not all of these traditional ideas are didactic in nature and are meant to inculcate certain virtues to individuals and discourage some vices abhorrent in societies.

Chiwanza (2021) adds that pre-colonial societies had reservoirs of priceless knowledge systems, which "were not written or codified as those of the colonisers – they were passed down from generation to generation through oral tradition." Muller (2002:409) cautions that archival scholars have a tendency to

> ...locate the idea of the "archive" in cultures with technologies of repetition, such as writing, sound recording, and film, and to use the word "memory" when dealing with "oral" or pre-literate communities. We conventionally think of archives as buildings, as monumental edifices to institutional or state power... Consequently, people with histories with documents that bear witness to earlier times have assumed greater positions of power than peoples without an easily recoverable past.

In writing about the value of the oral traditional religious music of the Shembe community in the KwaZulu-Natal province in South Africa, Muller (2002, p. 409–410) further argues that in order to counter "these conventions, I suggest that we begin to consider certain kinds of music composition as archival practice: as constituting valued sites for the deposit and retrieval of historical styles and practices in both literate and pre-literate contexts." These are some of the attempts that are now being made by decolonial scholars in trying to reinvent, repackage, re-archive, and present African knowledge to the epistemic arenas of the world. For example, Bhebhe (2018, p. 2) notes that "these traditional ideas embodied in Ndebele traditional literature cover every aspect of their life, such as religion, economic condition, political and social activities, including guidelines on sexual behaviour."

Therefore, it is imperative that in the contemporary era, the next generation of African archivists delve more into these pre-colonial archival practises in order to bridge the gap with the

Eurocentric knowledge systems that generated the colonial Anglo, Franco, and Luso archives that are now dominating the continent. In other words, indigenous archival systems existed in many forms long before the advent of colonisation in the African continent. However, that archive now faces annihilation from Christianity, Islam, modernism, westernism, globalisation, capitalism, African inferiorism, and other isms that tend to look down on African culture and traditions.

The archival landscape in Africa is still steeped in and reflective of colonial archives, which mainly speak to the history of the colonialists, as Tough (2009, p. 1) observes that "the colonial archives have excluded the voices of natives in their holdings." However, this cannot be treated as a surprise because these colonial archives were solely developed for the white community and its administrators. After many countries in Africa got their independence, there was a clamour and fervent movement to decolonise the archives. By decolonising the archives, the triumphant liberation nationalists meant the collection of the black content which can be kept in the white archive left by the colonialists. This is also the period when colonial white iconography was being removed and replaced by a black African one. However, the word decolonisation lends itself to contradictions. For example, how does one decolonise something that was never meant for them? Or are we saying that this colonial institution called the archive is part of a larger African heritage (or archive) which was abused by the colonialists who decided to solely use it for their memory only? These questions are meant to prick our minds into realising that sometimes, the colonial vestiges left behind by colonialists were never intended for Africans, but rather were their Western way of life and worldview. So why do we have to worry that these colonial archives left behind by the colonialists are silent about the black population? Ngoepe (2022, p. 5) also concurs by stating that "rather than focusing on decolonisation, perhaps we should consider starting on a clean slate and focussing on (re)Africanisation. Decolonisation would otherwise mean we are focusing on standards set by the West."

Archives are meant to preserve memory. If we speak about decolonisation instead of (re)Africanisation, what are we saying about African oral traditions, family praises, nomenclatures, and rock art paintings, which were and are still the granaries of the continent's history, culture, and traditions up to today? Are the sources of African memory not in the oral traditions such as izaga (proverbs), amalibho (riddles), inganekwane (folktales), and izangelo and Izibongo Zamakhosi (clan and king praise poems)? It is undeniable that these reservoirs of African memory, history, culture, and traditions are a point of reference to those who still believe in the African ways of doing things. Magoqwana (2018) talks about the isiXhosa concept of *umaKhulu* (this concept is based on the role played by our African grandmothers in bringing up their grandchildren). This *umaKhulu* concept, as explained and summarised by Magoqwana (2018:8) that "positions *uMakhulu* as an institution of knowledge that transfers not only 'history' through *iintsomi* (folktales), but also as a body of indigenous knowledge that stores, transfers, and disseminates knowledge and values." Further elucidating on this *uMakhulu* concept, Magoqwana and Adesina (2020:18) aver that

> UMakhulu is in herself, an essential institution to the sustenance of our environment, spiritual and economic makeup. She provides a critical untapped formal model of organising knowledge in an accessible and restorative manner. As a form of pedagogy, uMakhulu helps us to deal with enduring challenges that have shaped our 'body of knowledge' as she contributes towards imagining innovative ways of acquiring knowledge.

Are these archives not the ones we should be reviving and promoting? In decolonising the colonial archive, there is the need to avoid seeking Western epistemologies' equivalents and view African ways of knowing as standing on their own pedestals, as it is argued here about how the African cosmology was being preserved. As noted by Cook (1997), the differing epistemologies of the West and those of Africa are now forcing some "archivists in developing countries to seriously question whether classic archival concepts that emerged from the written culture of European bureaucracies are appropriate for preserving the memories of oral culture." Cook (1997) goes to the extent of even encouraging archivists to treat archival theory as "constantly evolving, ever mutating as it adapts to radical changes in the nature of records, record-creating organisations, record-keeping systems, record uses, and the wider cultural, legal, technological, social, and philosophical trends in society," hence the suggested conceptualisation of

Decolonisation or (re)Africanisation of archives? 47

indigenous archives in Chapter One. Lowry and MacNeil (2021) take note of the richness and value of the African archive and bemoan the Eurocentric-archival theories that close the door to such knowledge. Lowry and MacNeil (2021, p. 1) observe that in the field of archival studies in the West, nothing much has been done "to trouble its origin story, which recites a lineage of ideas that come down to us through the texts of Muller, Feith and Fruin, Jenkinson and Schellenberg." Lastly, they call for the recognition and validation of different stories about our intellectual past(s); stories that help us see the present and future differently by casting the past in a new light (Lowry & MacNeil, 2021, p. 1).

Then, the question asked by the authors of this book is whether to decolonise archives and their still extant systems of records appraisal, management, and access that were left behind by white imperialists, or to revive our own traditional archives that still face extinction because of globalisation, Western modernity, and coloniality. The African knowledge/archival system has been "neglected and categorised as irrational, primitive, even 'barbaric' and not science. This is despite the fact that this kind of knowledge has been used to heal and locate misfortune and suffering in different African societies" (Magoqwana & Adesina, 2020, p. 19). Ngugi wa Thiongo'o (1986) gives us the answer to why the global north has bastardised the African archive by arguing that

> the effect of the cultural bomb is to annihilate a people's belief in their names, their languages, in their environment, in their heritage of struggle, in their unity, in their capacities and ultimately in themselves. It makes them see their past as one wasteland of non-achievement and it makes them want to distance themselves from the wasteland...The intended results are despair, despondency and a collective death wish. Amidst this wasteland which it created, imperialism presents itself as the cure.

Is decolonisation the cure? The authors of this book believe that if decolonisation is not approached with a deep criticality towards the archival precepts that permeate every aspect of the archive as it is currently configured, it will result in coloniality reconfigured because it is still based on Western epistemologies. In other words, the argument is that archives in their Western form are a component of the knowledge systems of the Global North. Decolonising them to serve previously marginalised Africans – bringing the African into the archive, in other words, seeking black representation in the still-colonial archive – would be a continuation of ensnaring black people in the infrastructures of Western epistemology. In the same way that Aarons, Bastian and Griffin (2022) propose the 'caribbeanization of archives' in their book *Archiving Caribbean Identity*, we advocate for more than just the decolonisation of archives left by white imperialists, we also advocate for the appreciation of African knowledge systems and their preservation in their embedded traditional ways. This chapter advocates for the Africanisation of 'archives' as a concept, as institutions, and as practices, rather than for the representation of politics of archival decolonisation as it is so often approached today.

The empire's archive in the African continent

The colonial governments were very ardent record-keepers because their legal and administrative systems depended on written records, and archives were a component of these systems. Bishi (2020, p. 3) notes that "in the course of their administration, white colonial bureaucrats, politicians, clergymen and their metropolitan counterparts all produced records, archives, manuscripts and state-sanctioned publications." This primacy of written archives in the colonial mind relegated oral African memory practices to the periphery, if they were recognised as archival at all. As stated by Rayan (2021, p. 117), "symbolically annihilating the epistemologies of the colonised through record creation and archival description works to inscribe the hierarchy of the colonizer's truth over the counternarratives of the colonized." There is a strong interconnection between colonialism and Western archival methodology. Genovese (2016, p. 34) explicitly links colonialism and modern archival methodology by discoursing that "it is undeniable that the spread of colonialism – as well as the establishment and perpetuation of Western hierarchical models of power – went hand in hand with the development of archival methodology." Genovese (2016, p. 34) further concludes that this connection between colonialism and Western archival methodology was exacerbated by the imperialist grip on power by controlling and monopolising information to the extent of deliberately creating archival gaps when it came to the indigenous populations.

Where the colonised were documented, it was on the basis of using those records to show how to rule the 'native,' Murambiwa, Ngulube, Masuku and Sigauke (2012, p. 8) express this when they say, "…in essence, the African story was largely neglected unless it had incidental or circumstantial relevance to the colonial occupation of the country." In other words, the colonial archives became a prima facie case of how archival holdings in most situations are "a voice for the prominent, the conquerors, the vanquishers, the elites, the educated, whereas the voices of the grass-roots people, the defeated, the minorities, and the women were side-lined and forgotten" (Bhebhe, 2015, p. 44). Unfortunately, the postcolonial archive has also fallen into this trap, reinforcing the dictum that archives are always about memorialising those in power in order to legitimise their authority (Bhebhe & Ngoepe, 2021).

The colonial archive with reference to the blacks was mainly concentrated on native administration. Bishi (2014, p. 92–94) argues that "what we have now as a colonial archive is a collection of what officials desired to be collected mainly for administrative purposes" and that its continued use "perpetuates the coloniality of the colonial mind through documents." The paucity of records pertaining to blacks in the colonial archival repositories is lamented again by Namhila (2016, p.111), who opines that

> it has been observed that the institution where such records should be expected, the National Archives of Namibia, often cannot retrieve person-related records of persons previously classified as non-white under colonial and apartheid laws. Many native Namibians end up losing property or having problems claiming their constitutional rights due to a lack of evidence.

Evans (2017, p. x), in his book *Speeches that Shaped South Africa*, observed how difficult it was to obtain speeches made by African nationalists due to the imbalance in archiving during the apartheid era. Evans (2017, p. x) continues to bemoan the fact that "many apartheid leaders' words were carefully and systematically recorded as part of the Afrikaner nationalist project to build a nation from words... This was not always true of liberation movement discourse...." This dissatisfaction with the apartheid archive in terms of archiving black voices is audible when Evans (2017, p. xi) questions why even major speeches referred to in popular accounts of important events remained elusive. Ngoyi's keynote speech at the 1956 Women's March appears to have been lost. Saleh (2017, p. 2) precisely describes the apartheid archive as follows:

> Apartheid as an ideology for over almost half a century managed to exercise control over memory institutions and included a narrative that celebrated the rise to power of the Afrikaner. An example of this is that public holidays included 6 April which was Founder's Day – it was the day that Jan van Riebeeck arrived in South Africa in 1652; 31 May was celebrated as Republic Day, and 16 December was Day of the Covenant or Day of the Vow – the day in which a small Afrikaner force defeated about 20 000 Zulus at the Battle of the Blood River.

The paucity of archives pertaining to African activities is not limited to politics and leadership. Ngoepe and Ngulube (2014) lament archive repositories that failed to preserve memories of major African Independent Churches, such as the Zion Christian Church, which split in 1949. Despite the fact that such a split was resolved in court, there are no official court or police records.

The archives and museums that deal with black people in colonial archive repositories were mainly of racist anthropological nature, as put by Ndlovu and Hlongwane (2021, p. ix) that

> in colonial Southern Africa, for example, colonialists and their contacts in Europe were obsessed with the culture of the 'other,' the 'unfamiliar' cultural objects, including the collection of body parts and human remains of indigenous people in the pursuit of 'racial science'...

An example of this bizarre scientific racism is noted by Kotze and Ndhlovu (2021, p. 8), who state that one of the most notable fascinations of scientists of the "pure" "Khoisan was the difference in their physical attributes, specifically their genitalia." Hence, the abuse of Sarah Baartman, who was paraded in Europe just because of her physical looks. Even after her death, her remains were kept in the Museum of Man in Paris for the general public to see. Therefore, the blacks never celebrated in colonial archives and museums, but they became spaces where the black race was demonised, barbarised as savages, stripped of dignity, and reduced to objects of lewd racial fascination. The calls for colonial archive decolonisation, therefore, come as no surprise, and one of the solutions is for the Africans to create their own African archive along with the colonial archive, which tells the history of the black person. This solution is also recommended by Setumu (2015), who recommends that "the stories of Africans would be given validity and prominence by Africans themselves as the 'lions' and 'lionesses' would be determining and writing their own stories as opposed to the story coming from the hunter's perspective." How this is done matters if we are to resist augmenting the white archive.

Postcolonial archiving

Nothing much has changed for the colonial archive even after African countries got their independence. The colonial archive in the postcolonial context has remained Eurocentric in shape and form. Only patches of African stories here and there in a white archive have been done. The postcolonial archive is still frequented by the white population, even after African independences, because there is nothing much on indigenous stories (Bhebhe 2019). This section has been shortened deliberately, symbolically showing that there is nothing much to write about the postcolonial archive because it is just a continuation of the colonial archive, the only difference being that it is now managed by a black government. The following section discusses approaches that can be used in decolonising the colonial archive. Some of these approaches are the repatriation migrated archives, archival redescription, and community archives, among others.

Decolonisation of the archive

When African countries gained independence, they pushed for the decolonisation of the archives, galleries, and museums. This push was necessitated by the fact that "due to its central position in Western epistemology and the role it played in colonization, the archive has become a recurrent target for disruption" (Ernst,

2016, p. 86). This was in recognition of the fact that museums, galleries, and archives are not just places where old records and artefacts are dumped but are areas in which epistemic wars are being waged. The colonial archive was viewed as devoid of black stories, but it also had gaping holes left intentionally by retreating colonial masters, a process that some scholars, such as Elkins and Shepard, refer to as violent archiving. Therefore, this violent colonial archive can also be decolonised violently, whether that violence is physical, cosmological, or epistemological. Fanon ([1961] translated by Farrington, 2001, p. 1), observes that "decolonisation is always a violent event," keeping in mind that violence always begets violence. This violent archiving is a "reference to the destruction of archives by colonial state officials on their impending retreat" (Mir, 2015, p. 848). This phenomenon of violent archiving has mutated into the concept of migrated archives. This prompted some decolonial scholars, such as Grey (2019), to view the repatriation of the migrated archive as part of decolonisation. Grey (2019, p. 12) argues that "Indigenous repatriation is an opportunity to right historical wrongs, to remedy settler colonial violations, and to build new nation-to-nation relationships with Indigenous peoples." However, Garaba (2021, p. 1) is of the view that

> we need to start afresh and forget about the genre of migrated archives and focus the talks on de-colonisation/refiguring or Africanisation of archives because there is over-documentation of the colonial record in our repositories and these records are often biased or incorrect.

Africa is now 'free' from colonial powers, with Ghana being the first, South Africa getting its independence in 1994, Zimbabwe in 1980, and the newest nation being South Sudan on 9 July 2011. Can we then say decolonisation efforts have been successful so far? The contested answer to that question may be a big "No," because most of the national archives remain detached from the black population. Their archival services are still mostly frequented by the former colonisers and their generations. The authors of this book then ask whether this frenzy about decolonisation of archives is worth it because there is nothing much on the ground to show. It then becomes imperative to think of other ways, one of which is to resurrect the black archive, defined by Kumalo (2020, p. 30) as the black/indigenous epistemic traditions. This does not mean that the postcolonial governments should ignore the Western epistemologies but as the authors of this book, we propose that both worldviews should be acknowledged and treated on the same pedestal and, where possible, the black archive should take the lead in the African context. In other words, pluriversity, as defined by Mbembe (n.d., p. 19), should be the order of the day in the archival space. The same sentiments are echoed by Ernst (2016, p. 87), who mentions that "reclaiming history by introducing multivocality is an essential part of the decolonizing process." Fraser and Todd (2016, p. 33) argue that "to decolonise the archives requires an erasure or negation of the colonial realities of the archives themselves."

Generally, several different strategies for decolonising the colonial archives have been proposed. However, it should be noted that before discussing archive decolonisation, it is critical to recognise that

> archival decolonization starts by recognizing the harms of colonization and the imbrication of archival theory and practice within colonial mentalities, and then proceeds to identify ways of reducing those harms and rendering archives a tool that might advance the decolonizing and anticolonial agendas of Indigenous communities and individuals (Bak, 2021, p. 424).

Some scholars, such as Frederick (2019, p. 14–22), advocate for the decolonisation of collection-related terms and names. This could be relevant in some archival collections where liberation freedom fighters are referred to as terrorists in archival descriptions. Another example is traditional medicine healers, also known as witch doctors. Even some derogatory colonial names, such as kaffir, appear and persist in archival descriptions. Payne (2021, p. 28) expresses similar sentiments when she claims that

> for archival descriptions, for example, this may mean re-description that addresses racist language and ideology, while ensuring that the original descriptions are kept so that past societal and institutional racism cannot be erased. This approach would address harm in an immediate way but does

not necessarily shift the uneven power structures that led to racist description practices; as such, it only represents part of the work that needs to be done.

Others, however, may regard this as a violation of provenance and de fond archival principles, prompting Payne (2021, p. 31) to argue that "it is also imperative that archivists find ways to do this in a way that does not erase how archives have been complicit in the upholding of colonial power since their beginnings on settler colonial land...." Such challenges prompt other scholars to question whether it is even possible to deconstruct colonial construction practices. According to Frederick (2019, p. 20), if it is not possible to decolonise colonial construction practices, community archiving may be the solution for those affected groups of people.

Genovese (2016, p. 34) proposes that for archival decolonisation to be achieved, there is a need for archivists to adopt activism skills because "the time has come for the archivist to see activism as part of their job description in order to reform a former catalyst of colonialism, the archive." Hence, there is a need for archivists to understand that there is no neutrality about an archive but all about the politics of knowledge. Therefore, there is a need for them to also understand the archive in a political manner; hence, the call for archival activism. Genovese (2016, p. 40) suggests that "there must also be a protracted effort to understand and incorporate Indigenous ways of knowing and epistemologies within information science programmes in order to combat a Western-dominated approach to archival science." This statement by Genovese (2016) should also be applied to African archivists to come up with archival theories that speak to the African archival challenges that were created by the Eurocentric archival methodologies. It is very unfortunate that there is still a lack of African archivists who can theorise the African archive and come up with African solutions. Instead of theorising the African archive prior to colonisation, in taking note of African epistemologies, particularly how they valued orality, the current crop of African archivists has done otherwise, becoming merely an appendage of Eurocentric archival methodologies, a situation exacerbated by imbibing Westernised archival curriculum. However, due to the Rhodes Must Fall movement, which led to the manifestation of the decolonisation of the African university's curriculum, especially in South Africa, there is hope. Records and archival management departments should ride on that movement and decolonise their curriculum so that they address the neglect of African ontologies and epistemologies. In other words, the decolonisation of the colonial archive in Africa should begin at university level, with a radical review of the archival curriculum that takes into account African epistemologies and ontologies. There might be a need to avoid constructing a universal model of archival science as a discipline because, currently, archival science in most of the third-world countries or in the global south just replicates the Western archival epistemologies which reinforce civilising missions over local indigenous histories and archival practices (Clarke, 2021, p. 271).

According to Hendrickson (2017, p. 321), decolonisation of the archive can imply the preservation and allowing of the booming of the 'other' archive alongside the 'national archive.' This can be accomplished by bringing the archive to the street, as suggested by the murals in Chapter One. Hendrickson (2017, p. 321) adds weight to this argument by claiming that

> yet an alternative archive of events exists if we take our research to the "streets"– that is, incorporate personal archives and oral histories – to create a transnational and post imperial archive. With this alternative archive, perhaps historians cannot only liberate Mai 68 from the confines of a nation-bound event but also consider the role that archives, stories, and remembrances play in the larger processes of decolonization.

In other words, the colonial or even postcolonial conventional archive can be left intact without trying to change it, whilst the decolonised archive is created alongside it. This approach may even be favoured by scholars who view direct disruption of the colonial archive as anti-provenance and totally against the theoretical foundations of these Eurocentric structures. Some scholars, such as Fraser and Todd (2016), are very sceptical about whether archives can be decolonised in the first place. Hence, they propose what they call a historically informed approach. In their own words, Fraser and Todd (2016, p. 33) argue that "given the inherent colonial realities of the archives as institutions, any effort to decolonise or Indigenise the archives in Canada can therefore only ever be partial." Fraser and Todd (2016, p. 33) put forward that "acknowledging the inherent colonial paradigms that inform and shape the archives as institutions, we propose moving away from the question of decolonising the archives themselves and suggest instead applying a historically-informed." It appears by this they mean that "the application of a decolonial sensibility is necessary to attend to the complex relationships between archives and Indigenous peoples. Making archives friendlier to Indigenous people and pursuits."

It is like how much we try, these Eurocentric centres of knowledge would remain combative to the other ways of knowing such as Africanism because, by their very nature, they are "knowledge producers and discursive gatekeepers rather than simply as storage facilities for facts about our pasts" (Hendrickson, 2017, p. 321). Therefore, what this means is that the decolonised archives can be constructed in the form of community archives. They can again be constructed as personal archives, as suggested by Hendrickson (2017), especially for those figures who were viewed as too left to be accommodated by the ruling regimes. Bak (2021, p. 420) shares these same sentiments, as he postulates that

> Helen Samuels sought to document institutions in society by adding to official archives counterweights of private records and archivist-created records such as oral histories. In this way, she recognised and sought to mitigate biases that arise from the institution-centric application of archival functionalism.

There appears to be "no single approach to decolonising or Indigenising the archives. It will necessitate nuanced, thoughtful, and contextual approaches that take into account specific relationships, locations, histories, and legal and political realities" (Fraser & Todd, 2016, p. 38). Oral history has been one of the subaltern's methods for infiltrating the archival epistemic and prop in their voices. As a result, it may be a method that can be used to decolonise the colonial archive. Fraser and Todd (2016, p. 38) support this approach, stating that

> one way of bringing greater diversity to archival spaces and featuring Indigenous voices is to prioritise and expand historical collections to include a greater number and range of oral

history, whether in the form of transcripts, audio or video files, or previously published works.

Alternatively, as suggested in Chapter One, archives can be reconstructed through murals, rock art paintings, and orality.

Can (re)Africanisation of the archive be the answer to the faltering decoloniality?

(Re)Africanisation is a much deeper epistemological project than decolonisation. In the archival context, it speaks to the importance of African ways of knowing and the didactic value of the continent's cultures and traditions. The section in this chapter on African archiving before the great invasion by the imperialists shows how significant and central this archive is. Falola (2017) describes this as the African ritual archive. Gray, Kreitzer and Mupedziswa (2014, p. 104) argue that "Africanisation, Africology, and Africentrism were more than concepts and philosophies, they were political projects aimed at cultural recovery and empowerment." Therefore, the Africentric frame of reference has become an instrument of "critique... of the dis-location caused by the cultural, economic and political domination of Europe" (Asante, 1999, p. 7) and 'correction,' reorienting Africans to their cultural roots and heritage (Gray et al., 2014, p. 104). What this means is that there is a need for the archivists in Africa to retrace their steps back to the African ritual archive as described by Falola (2017). This theoretical conceptualisation which favours Africanisation over decolonisation is driven by the fact that decolonisation is becoming more of just patching the colonial archive that was left by the colonialists but without any significant epistemological changes. In museology, decolonisation has just been shifting, moving around of artifacts, and adding some pieces that speak to the African story. The same applies to the archives in which the colonial archive has remained intact, and decolonisation has not changed anything much other than to add archival material that speaks to the Africans. In other words, it appears decolonisation is faltering; therefore, it may be time that the archivists in Africa consider ditching this colonial archive in favour of our African ritual archive, as some might think. However, this is not that easy because the idea of an African identity and culture, which is a single, homogeneous monolithic, is potentially misleading in the sense that Africa has imbibed some epistemologies that can simply be not shaken off. Maybe African archivists may consider a watered-down Africanisation, which is defined by Makgoba (1997, p. 199) as not being about expelling Europeans and their cultures, but about affirming African culture and their identity in a world community, a process of inclusion, not exclusion. How this watered Africanised archive may look, can always be debated, but Chapter Seven of this book tries to answer that question.

Conclusion

Decolonisation of archives should be carefully considered before implementation, as it can easily lead to other failed isms. It is easily appropriated and manipulated by postcolonial authoritarian regimes in their quest to use public archives to anoint themselves as legitimate rulers, thus perpetuating the tendencies that were prevalent in the colonial archive. As a result, Ngoepe (2022) contends that even after (re)Africanisation, Eurocentric thinking can take centre stage, resulting in those who should be beneficiaries becoming gate-crashers prevented by gatekeepers who would have taken their birth right. As a result, it has been suggested in this chapter that decolonising the colonial archive by removing and adding archives may be counterproductive because the archive as an epistemological arena is not decolonised. While archival repatriation and re-description of colonial archives have been proposed as alternative approaches to decolonisation, the recommendations made are the re-invention, re-use, and promotion of the oral African archive, which is embodied in African traditional literature such as ads riddles, proverbs, and folktales, among others, as well as murals on the wall, and rock art paintings. The creation of a decolonised archive in the form of community and personal archives that run parallel with the colonial archive has also been proposed and recommended.

Note

1 Mbuyiswa Makhuba is a South African anti-Apartheid student activist who is best known through carrying Hector Pietersen in a photograph

taken by Sam Nzima after Pietersen was shot during the Soweto Uprising in 1976.

References

Aarons, J., Bastian, J.A. and Griffin, S.H. (2022). *Archiving Caribbean identity*. 1st ed. London: Routledge.
Adesina, J.O. (2006). Sociology beyond despair: recovery of nerve, endogeneity, and epistemic intervention. *South African Review of Sociology*, 37(2): 241–249.
Asante, M.K. (1999). *The painful demise of Eurocentrism: an Afrocentric response to critics*. Trenton, NJ: Africa World Press.
Bak, G. (2021). Counterweight: Helen Samuels, archival decolonization, and social license. *The American Archivist* 84(2): Fall/Winter: 421–444.
Bhebhe, S. (2015). Description of the oral history programme at the National Archives of Zimbabwe. *Oral History Australia Journal*, 37: 49–55.
Bhebhe, S. (2018). Interrogating myths surrounding sex education in Zimbabwean schools: lessons to be learned from Ndebele Traditional Literature/Oral Traditions. *Oral History Journal of South Africa*, 6(1): 1–18.
Bhebhe, S. (2019). Memorialising minority groups in post-independence Zimbabwe and South Africa: A critical analysis of oral history programme. Doctor of Philosophy in the subject of Information Science at the University of South Africa, Pretoria.
Bhebhe, S. and Ngoepe, M. (2021). Elitism in critical emancipatory paradigm: national archival oral history collection in Zimbabwe and South Africa. *Archival Science*, 21: 155–172, http://doi.org/10.1007/s10 502- 020-09351-y
Bishi, G. (2014). The colonial archive and contemporary chieftainship claims: the case of Zimbabwe, 1935 to 2014. MA Dissertation, Bloemfontein: University of the Free State. Available at: https://scholar.ufs.ac.za/bitstream/handle/11660/2352/BishiG.pdf?sequence=1&is Allowed=y (Accessed 1 April 2022).
Bishi, G. (2020). *Uncovering 'undesirable whites' in the colonial archive*. Available at: https://africasacountry.com/2020/05/uncovering-undesirable-whites-in-the-colonial-archive/ (Accessed 15 May 2022).
Callinicos, L. and Odendaal, A. (1996). Report on archives in South Africa by Luli Callinicos and Andre Odendaal, convenors of the Archives Sub-Committee of the Arts and Culture Task Group (ACTAG). *SA Archives Journal*, 38: 33–49.
Carruthers, W. (2019). Heritage, preservation, and decolonization: entanglements, consequences, action? *Future Anterior*, 16(2): ii–xxiv. Available at: https://muse.jhu.edu/article/785268 (Accessed 31 March 2022).

Chiwanza, T.H. (2021). The truth about African civilizations before colonial invasion. *Orinoco Tribune*, November 24. Available at: https://orinocotribune.com/the-truth-about-african-civilizations-before-colonial-invasion/ (Accessed 1 April 2022).

Clarke, K. (2021). Reimagining social work ancestry: toward epistemic decolonization. *Affilia: Feminist Inquiry in Social Work*, 37(2): 266–278. doi:10.1177/08861099211051326

Cook, T. (1997). What is past is prologue: a history of archival ideas since 1898, and the future paradigm shift. *Archivaria*, 43 (Spring). Available at: archivaria.ca/index.php/archivaria/article/view/12175/13184 (Accessed 10 April 2022).

Davidson, B. (1964). *The African past-chronicles from antiquity to modern times*. London: Penguin Books Ltd.

Ernst, S.A. (2016). Going beyond the archival grid: Carl Beam and Greg Curnoe's decolonization of a colonizing space. *World Art*, 6(1): 85–102. doi:10.1080/21500894.2016.1162843

Evans, M. (2017). *Speeches that shaped South Africa: From Malan to Malema*. Cape Town: Penguin Books.

Falola, T. (2017). Ritual archive. In A. Afolayan and T. Falola. (Eds.), *The Palgrave handbook of African philosophy*. London: Palgrave Macmillan.

Fanon, F. (2001). *The wretched of the earth*, trans. Constance Farrington. London: Penguin Classics.

Fraser, C. and Todd, Z. (2016). Decolonial sensibilities: indigenous research and engaging with archives in contemporary colonial Canada. Available at: *L'Internationale*. www.internationaleonline.org/research/decolonising_practices/54_decolonial_sensibilities_indigenous_research_and_engaging_with_archives_in_contemporary_colonial_canada/ (Accessed 12 April 2022).

Frederick, S. (2019). Decolonization in the archives: at the item level. *iJournal*, 4(2): 14–22. Available at: https://theijournal.ca/index.php/ijournal/article/view/32554/25023 (Accessed 15 July 2022).

Garaba, F. (2021). Migrated archives: time for closure to turn the wheels of reconciliation and healing for Africa. *Journal of South African Society of Archivists*, 54: 1–12.

Genovese, T.R. (2016). Decolonizing archival methodology: combating hegemony and moving towards a collaborative archival environment. *Alternative*, 12(1). https://doi.org/10.20507/AlterNative.2016.12.1.3

Ghaddar, J.J. (2021). Total archives for land, law and sovereignty in settler Canada. *Archival Science*, 21: 59–82.

Gray, M., Kreitzer, L. and Mupedziswa, R. (2014) The enduring relevance of indigenisation in African social work: a critical reflection on ASWEA's legacy, *Ethics and Social Welfare*, 8(2): 101–116. doi:10.1080/17496535.2014.895397

Grey, R.R.R. (2019). Repatriation and decolonization: thoughts on ownership, access, and control. In F. Gunderson, C. Robert, R.C. Lancefield and B. Woods. (Eds,), *The Oxford handbook of musical repatriation*. Oxford: Oxford University Press. doi:10.1093/oxfordhb/9780190659806.013.39

Hegel, G.W.F. (1956). *This philosophy of history*. Dover Publications.

Heissig, W. and Schott, R. (1998). The present-day importance of oral traditions – their preservation, publication and indexing. In W. Heissig and R. Schott. (Eds.), *Die heutige Bedeutung oraler Traditionen / The Present-Day Importance of Oral Traditions*. Abhandlungen der Nordrhein-Westfälischen Akademie der Wissenchaften, 102. VS Verlag für Sozialwissenschaften. https://doi.org/10.1007/978-3-322-83676-2_2

Hendrickson, B. (2017). From the archives to the streets: listening to the global 1960s in the former French Empire. *French Historical Studies*, 40(2): 319–342. doi:10.1215/00161071-3761643

Jackson, S. (2020). Decolonizing archives in the digital ge. In R. Somers Miles, A. Osbourne, E. Tzialli, and E. Captain. (Eds.). *Inward outward, critical archival engagements with sounds and films of coloniality*. Inward Outward, pp. 13–20. doi:10.18146/inout2020

Ketelaar, E. (1992). Archives of the people, by the people, for the people. *SA Archives Journal*, 34: 5–16.

Kotze, A. and Ndhlovu, B. (2021). Subjugation, exposure and healing: Human remains, museums and indigenous communities. In S.M. Ndlovu and A.K. Hlongwane (Eds.), Public history, heritage and culture in South Africa: the struggle continues. Johannesburg: Skotaville Publishing, pp. 1–32.

Kumalo, S.H. (2020). Resurrecting the Black Archive through the decolonisation of philosophy in South Africa. *Third World Thematics: A TWQ Journal*, 5: 1–2, 19–36, doi:10.1080/23802014.2020.1798276

Letsekha, T. (2013). Revisiting the debate on the Africanisation of higher education: an appeal for a conceptual shift. *Independent Journal of Teaching and Learning*, 8: 5–18.

Linebaugh, R. and Lowry, J. (2021). The archival colour line: race, records and post-colonial custody. *Archives and Records*, 42(3): 284–303. doi:10.1080/23257962.2021.1940898

Lowry, J. and MacNeil, H. (2021). Archival thinking: archaeologies and genealogies. *Archival Science*, 21: 1–6. https://doi.org/10.1007/s10502-020-09355-8

Magoqwana, B. (2018). *Repositioning uMakhulu as an institution of knowledge: beyond 'biologism' towards uMakhulu as the body of the indigenous knowledge*. Available at: https://mg.co.za/tag/repositioning-umakhulu-as-an-institution-of-knowledge-beyond-biologism/ (Accessed 3 January 2022).

Magoqwana, B. and Adesina, J. (2020). Reconnecting African sociology to the mother: towards a woman-centred endogenous sociology in South Africa. *African Sociological Review*, 24(2): 4–24. Available at: www.jstor.org/stable/10.2307/48630990 (Accessed 5 January 2022).

Makgoba, M. (1997). *Mokoko: the Makgoba affair – a reflection on transformation*. Florida: Vivlia.

Matshotshwane, J. and Ngoepe, M. (2022). Transcending invisible lanes through inclusion of sports memories in archival system in South Africa. *HTS Teologiese Studies/ Theological Studies*, 78(3): 6.

Mbembe, A. (n.d). Decolonizing knowledge and the question of the archive. Available at: https://wiser.wits.ac.za/system/files/Achille%20Mbembe%20-%20Decolonizing% 20Knowledge%20and%20the%20 Question%20of%20the%20Archive.pdf (Accessed 2 May 2022).

Mir, F. (2015). AHR round table: The archives of decolonisation. *American Historical Review*, 120(3): 844–851, www.libs.uga.edu/reserves/docs/main-spring2019/palmer-hist7900/2/mir-the-archives-of-decolonization.pdf (Accessed 10 May 2022).

Muller, C. (2002). Archiving Africanness in sacred song. *Ethnomusicology*, 46(3): 409–431. Available at: www.jstor.org/stable/852717 (Accessed 2 April 2022).

Murambiwa, I.M., Ngulube, P., Masuku, M. and Sigauke, D.T. (2012). Archival development in Zimbabwe 1935-2010: Setting the scene. In P. Ngulube (Ed.), *National Archives 75@30: 75 years of archiving excellence at the National Archives of Zimbabwe*. Harare: Zimbabwe: National Archives of Zimbabwe, pp. 1–20.

Namhila, E.N. (2016). Content and use of colonial archives: an under-researched issue. *Archival Science*, 16: 111–123. DOI 10.1007/s10502-014-9234-0

Ndlovu, S.M. and Hlongwane, A.K (Eds.) (2021). *Public history, heritage and culture in South Africa: the struggle continues*. Johannesburg: Skotaville Publishing.

Ngoepe, M. (2009). End apartheid legacy by naming black people. *Sowetan*. 19 June.

Ngoepe, M. (2019). Archives without archives: A window of opportunity to build inclusive archive in South Africa. *Journal of the South African Society of Archivists*, 52: 149–166.

Ngoepe, M. (2022). Neither prelegal nor nonlegal: Oral memory in troubled times. *HTS Teologiese Studies/Theological Studies*, 78(3): a7533. https://doi.org/10.4102/hts.v78i3.7533

Ngoepe, M. and Ngulube, P. (2014). Eternal memory or holy amnesia? Preservation of, and access to records and archives of African Independent Churches in South Africa. *ESARBICA Journal*, 33: 36–45.

Ngugi wa Thiong'o. (1986). *Decolonizing the mind: the politics of language in African literature*. Oxford: James Currey.

Ntsebeza, L. (2018). Introduction. In J. Bam, L. Ntsebeza and A. Zinn (Eds.), *Whose history counts: Decolonising African Pre-colonial historiography*. Cape Town: African Sun Media. Sun PReSS, pp. 1–12. https://doi.org/10.18820/9781928314127

Osundare, N. (1998). Squaring up to Africa's future: a writer's reflection on the predicament of a continent. In O. Oladipo (Ed.), *Remaking Africa: Challenges of the twenty-first century*. Ibadan, Nigeria: Hope Publications, pp. 228–235.

Payne, K. (2021). Archival harm reduction: utilizing public health harm reduction concepts for reconciliatory power shifts in archives. MA, Manitoba: Joint Master's Program University of Manitoba/University of Winnipeg Winnipeg, Manitoba. Available at: https://mspace.lib.umanitoba.ca/xmlui/bitstream/handle/1993/35762/Payne_Krystal.pdf?sequence=1&isAllowed=y (Accessed 15 May 2022).

Priya, S. (n.d). Colonial archives and state power: A historiographical enquiry, *South –Asian Journal of Multidisciplinary Studies*, 4(4): 1–9. Available at: www.academia.edu/34769441/COLONIAL_ARCHIVES_AND_STATE_POWER_A_HISTORIOGRAPHICAL_ENQUIRY (Accessed 15 May 2022).

Ramose, M.B. (1998). Foreword. In S. Seepe (Ed.), *Black perspectives on tertiary institutional transformation*. Johannesburg: Vivlia.

Rayan, T.N. (2021). Archival imperialism: examining Israel's Six Day War files in the era of "decolonization". [*Special issue on Unsettling the Archives.*] *Across the Disciplines*, 18(1/2): 108–121. https://doi.org/10.37514/ATD-J.2021.18.1-2.09

Saleh, R. (2017). *Archives, archiving and the marginalised: a reflection of South Africa*. Paper presented at: Arxius per la Democràcia i Dret a la Informació VIII Jornades de l'Associació d'Arxivers i Gestors de Documents Valencians València, 26–27 d'octubre de 2017.

Schwartz, J. and Cook, T. (2002). Archives, records, and power: the making of modern memory. *Archival Science*, 2: 1–19. Available at: https://pdfs.semanticscholar.org/e0d6/0de730ff149bd33b960291f12a307c219f03.pdf (Accessed 12 December 2021).

Seroto, J. (2011). Indigenous education during the pre-colonial period in Southern Africa. *Indilinga – African Journal of Indigenous Knowledge Systems*, 10(1): 77–88.

Setumu, T. (2015). Inclusion of rural communities in national archival and records system: a case study of Blouberg-Makgabeng-Senwabarwana area. *Journal of the African Society of Archivists*, 48: 34–44. Available at: www.ajol.info/index.php/jsasa/article/download/129270/118820 (Accessed 15 December 2021).

Tough, A.G. (2009). Archives in sub-Saharan Africa half a century after independence. Available at: link.springer.com/article/10.1007/s10502-009-9078-1 (Accessed 12 December 2021).

Trevor-Roper, H. (1967). *The rise of christian Europe.* London: Jarrold and Sons.

3 Authentication of indigenous archives

Introduction

Although the indigenous archives identified in Chapter One can be used as a tool to transform archival holdings, they have their limitations and salient problems. For example, oral history often has a limitation that misleads people into believing that it (oral history) automatically yields accurate renditions of past events. With oral memory, Setumu (2010, p. 20) identifies one of the problematic areas as "unreliability of memory, deliberate falsification, unfairness through vindictiveness, excessive discretion, superficiality, and gossip; oversimplification, distortion of the interviewee's role; lack of perspective, distortion due to personal feelings, self-consciousness, influence of hindsight, and repetition of published evidence." However, Tough (2012) observes that it should be noted that written records do reflect the worldviews and personal prejudices of their creators. Such records are open to alteration, manipulation, and subjectivity, as they can be used to further the writer's own agenda, as with their oral counterparts (Hatang, 2000). Ngoepe (2012) gives an example of annual reports of governmental bodies in South Africa that paint a picture of public organisations that are performing well, contrary to what the Auditor-General of South Africa found in its audit reports. This shows that such reports are prepared to portray the positive image of the institutions rather than the true reflection of what transpired during a particular financial year. While there are service delivery protests and disclaimer audit opinions from the Auditor-General of South Africa, the reports always paint a positive picture of governmental bodies that are performing (Ngoepe,

DOI: 10.4324/9781003277989-4

2012). With oral memory, it is also possible that, in some instances, the truth can be distorted to suit the griot or that forgetfulness can lead to the problem of chronology of events. This, in turn, can compromise the reliability and authenticity of such oral memory, as evidence will be inconsistent due to different versions, as has been the case with some Independent African Churches, especially during squabbles for leadership (Ngoepe & Ngulube, 2014).

Therefore, organisations, communities, families, and individuals who are in possession or control of indigenous archives conceptualised in Chapter One may need guidance to authenticate or certify that such archives are accurate, reliable, and trustworthy. This will help to safeguard the authenticity of such memories. For the purpose of this chapter, we chose to use the word 'authentication' although it is currently understood in Western archival theory and has to do with concepts of diplomatics, a European science concerned with written records, as we feel it may also be applicable to indigenous archives. Given the preceding discussion of decolonisation and (re)Africanisation, we look at how we should rethink authentication. This may also augur well with an argument by Lowry (n.d.) regarding inversion of the archival threshold, where authentication is not achieved by transmission into the archive, but transmission out of it, into publicity. This is so because indigenous archives as described in this book are not in traditional archival space and they are openly available. In this way, it may be a transition to a new system of domination.

This chapter looks at how the identified indigenous archives, that is, oral memory, rock art paintings, and murals, are authenticated traditionally through corroboration. We opted for the term 'authentication' as it is used in the archival science field. It should be noted that the concept of indigenous archives has not been given opportunity to grow. We will describe how indigenous archives are authenticated traditionally. Furthermore, archival principles and disruptive technologies such as blockchain technology will be explored to see whether they can be used to authenticate these records. With regard to oral memory, the focus would be on the examples given in Chapter One, such as family praises. Furthermore, this chapter considers how these indigenous archives can be safeguarded. In archival theory, records on which the creator relies in the usual and ordinary course of business are presumed authentic. However, indigenous archives pose significant risks that such memories or rock art paintings will be altered, either inadvertently or intentionally. The form and media of indigenous archives are different from those of paper-based and digital records.

Protection of indigenous archives

The indigenous knowledge system has been protected in various ways since time immemorial. However, such ways have been hugely disrupted by colonialism. Interviews with heritage consultants suggest that, in many African traditions, the king or his delegated authority is the custodian and embodiment of culture. This includes what we discussed about indigenous archives. In our classification of indigenous archives, there are those that are at individual and family or clan level (family praises or nomenclature), community level (collective history of the community or nomenclature), and nation level (people falling under a particular king, not a country, e.g. Royal Bafokeng nation). The king as the custodian of such cultural heritage has rules that protect and safeguard his assets, including knowledge. The rules also extend to passers-by or whoever seeks refuge in the land of the king. As a result, subjects had much respect for their kings, as reflected in most of the philosophical statements and proverbs about royalty they adhere to.

Some of the adages in Northern Sotho that depict the power of the king include *Ke swana ya mošate, wa e gapa o a oba wa e tlogela o a oba*, literally meaning "it is a cow from the royal house, you herd it, you are wrong you pass it, you are wrong," but, figuratively, it may mean "damned if you do and damned if you don't." The proverb is laid upon the power of the royal family and the fear people have for the king. The proverb that is directly relevant in terms of protection of cultural heritage says *Lentšu la kgoši le agelwa morako* – meaning that the instruction of the king is always followed. In this regard, for example, the king can just give an instruction that the rock art paintings are not to be vandalised. Anyone who disobeys will be severely punished. Until colonialism disrupted the tradition, people would follow the instructions of the king and perpetrators were punished immediately.

The other way of protecting cultural heritage, including indigenous archives, was through taboos and ethical principles. For example, in the prologue of the book *History of Batlhaloga of Moloto Kingdom*, Letladi Moloto (2021), anthropologist and genealogical researcher, indicates that men and women who are the custodians of oral history are told history under oath never to alter, add, or subtract any word with the knowledge that anyone who thinks of changing any of the stories of his people would fall under a curse that covers him, his children, and his grandchildren. People would then always tell the truth to avoid such a curse. In general, the local people respect their heritage; they do not vandalise rock art paintings, as they consider them part of their lives and also for fear of being cursed.

However, colonialism and apartheid disrupted traditional rule to the extent that some kings who opposed white government systems and policies were severely punished, especially by being deposed while those who complied were handsomely rewarded and propped up. This resulted in some subjects being displaced, which also affected the knowledge systems of many communities. This is exacerbated by the fact that indigenous archives did not have the opportunity to grow; it was limited in scope to develop at its own pace and based on its own principles, as the colonial conquest introduced the Western archival system. Hence, many commentators advocate for their inclusion in mainstream archives. We believe that there are those that can be included such as those converted from oral history as a method, but not in its natural setting. Likewise, murals can be used to decolonise Western archives like the example given in Chapter One about the murals in the Letlamoreng Dam precinct in Mafikeng, South Africa's North West province, which are based on archival images displayed. The archive images displayed at the Letlamoreng Dam depict a line-up of the Barolong, an ethnic group in Mahikeng, as well as iconic figures who played critical leadership roles in Mahikeng, such as Sol Plaatjie, the African National Congress's first secretary general (1912–1915).

Due to disruption and the fact that indigenous archives have not been part of the curriculum for archival science until now, it might be worth considering whether techniques and principles of archival science can be used to authenticate indigenous archives. Duranti (1994) asserts that the preservation of both oral and digital memory requires a proactive effort, namely migration from one carrier to another. According to archival theory, in order to have records, we must have information (an understandable message) conveyed (created and used) in an accessible manner. According to Duranti (1994), memory is no different from any other medium of communication, and its storage function is just as reliable. In this regard, the information is saved and deemed valuable by its creator for future reference. It is necessary to have safeguards in place to ensure that the core message of the story is not lost, even when it is retold.

We believe that indigenous archives and written records can complement and intersect each other. According to Yeo (2019), written records arose as an attempt to overcome the limitations of human memory. Indeed, as Ngoepe (2020a) points out, when producing meeting minutes, oral deliberations are held until consensus is reached, resulting in recorded resolutions in the form of minutes. Turner (2012) contends that new information emerges orally before it appears in other formats, such as meeting minutes, which are recorded as an act to counteract human forgetfulness. Furthermore, as demonstrated in this chapter, written records can be transformed into murals, which serve as extended archives in this regard, while the original record is kept in the archive's repository. These murals, in turn, help to bring archives to the people while also preserving them because people will not be handling the actual archives but will instead be viewing the mural.

Authentication

The term 'authentication' refers to the process or action of proving or showing something to be true, genuine, or valid. In the InterPARES Trust Terminology, authentication is defined by Pearce-Moses (2019) as a declaration of a record's authenticity at a specific point in time by a juridical person entrusted with the authority to make such a declaration. When used as a verb, it means to declare, either orally, in writing, or by affixion of a seal, that an entity is what it purports to be, after verifying its identity (Pearce-Moses, 2019). In this chapter, we look at how indigenous archives identified are authenticated. These records also need to be authenticated to ensure they are trustworthy. Duranti (2009) contends that the trustworthiness of records needs to be tested using scientific methods. Trustworthiness is assessed based on the process of formation of documents and on their formal characteristics, structure, and transmission through time and space. The trustworthiness of a record includes its reliability (the trustworthiness of a document as a statement of fact, based on the competence of its author and the controls on its creation), accuracy (the correctness and precision of a document's content based on the competence of its author and the controls on content recording and transmission), and authenticity (the trustworthiness of a document that is what it purports to be, untampered with and uncorrupted based on identity and integrity). With paper-based and digital records, their authenticity can be tested using archival theories and technologies. Macdonald (1995) questions whether oral history can acquire the qualities of authenticity, as explained by Hilary Jenkinson in his canonical manual and other archival principles.

Several authors, such as Stancic, Ngoepe and Mukwevho (2019), as well as Ngoepe, Mukwevho and Mosweu (2022), have written about the authentication of digital records. Duranti (1994) and Ngoepe (2020a; 2022) have written extensively about the authentication of oral history as a record. Ngoepe (2020a, p. 315) divides oral history into two categories: the first as a research method for academic purposes in which oral historians, archivists, and scholars record histories from eyewitnesses or secondary participants, and the second as practiced by communities in traditional feasts for storytelling, displaying crests, performing songs, family praises, harvest festivals, weddings, and times of initiation. With the latter, oral history can be easily authenticated as every practice is witnessed by either a family, clan, or community member. However, where oral history is used as a method, Lekgwathi (2014) advises that the recorder should identify the problem of motive by asking questions about the informant's identity and their agendas (both public and hidden) in giving their accounts. Furthermore, contradictions are identified by cross-checking the informant's recollection against other oral accounts and archival sources in cases, where they are available. These issues require techniques for the authentication of indigenous archives. As the historical truth is not directly accessible, the two ways of indirectly accessing the past: witness testimony and the documentary truth represented by the written accounts of the facts and the material instruments of the acts can be used. In both cases, what we regard as truth will depend entirely on our trust in its source. Understanding whose truth we are dealing with requires using traditional archival principles, concepts, and methods. Here we are going to discuss how to authenticate orality (praise poems), murals, and rock art paintings.

Orality

Like liquid communication such as social media content, websites, and e-mails, oral history is fluid. "The fluid context of the text is inextricably linked to social situation, space, landscape, physical landmarks, and items of material culture," writes Harris (2000, p. 92), "and validates a collective's re-telling, re-vision, and re-interpretation of its narratives." Therefore, Harris (1997) views the recording of narrative and the archiving of orality as destroying the fluidity and contextual links and alienating the griot from the word. Instead, he advises that orality should not be conceptualised as memory waiting to be archived, but already as an archive. This brings to the fore the issue of oral history as a method and oral history happening in a natural setting. As a method, the researcher walks around with a tape recorder or any form of recording equipment, interviewing people, which produces oral history documents. In this regard, Macdonald (1995) questions whether archival theory, practices, and methods may apply to the authentication of oral history documents. The conclusion they make is that if a document does not have the characteristics of archival records, it may not necessarily be amenable to archival principles. Macdonald (1995) says that these kinds of recorded oral histories are true to the person who made them.

While we are not opposed to recording oral history, we view recorded oral history as a new form of record. Where we consider it as an original record, it is when oral history occurs in its natural setting and people have a conversation narrating their stories rather than somebody recording a story about them. When recording the stories, some of the activities happening around us may be missed, leaving only fragments of the activities. Even with photographs and other visual memories, the photographer may choose to record a portion of an event, and their point of view suggests an interpretation. In this regard, the equipment, social context, and intent of the photographer affect what photographs will be recorded, what will be printed, and how they will be presented to viewers. While oral memories are not neutral as they live in, on, and through people, these indigenous archives have meaning in the society that created them. Hence, the natural setting is important for authentication. In this regard, oral history such as family praises can be authenticated in the context of family gatherings or community feasts. As Ngoepe (2020a; 2022) would attest, this authentication works in a similar way to the blockchain technology principles. Ngoepe (2022) gives an example of how results were announced in school assemblies in the early 1980s at the end of the term; as such, schools did not have equipment such as typewriters and computers to capture results and produce individual transcripts. An announcement of the results in the general assembly would mean that learners and teachers present would later serve as witnesses as to who failed and who passed, if there is any dispute. This works the same way as blockchain technology, or rather, blockchain technology works the same way. It should, however, be noted that from time immemorial, this method of authentication has been used by indigenous people long before blockchain technology was invented.

Oral history such as family praise, stories, and traditional music conveying messages are mostly transmitted in groups in certain places (at night or during feasts). For example, Figure 3.1 reflects

Figure 3.1 Blouberg-Makgabeng-Senwabarwana cultural festival.

activities for a cultural festival where oral history in its natural setting is performed. This way, all the people who are present would serve as witnesses (chain), just like in blockchain technology, where all the previous witnesses are used in each transaction (event), making it increasingly harder to change the information because to do so, there is a need to conspire with all witnesses. Therefore, all people available could be considered witnesses, and they can always confirm the stories, the family praises, or whatever is being shared.

In the case of Delgamuukw v. British Columbia in Canada, the appellants, the Gitksan Houses have an "adaawk," which is a collection of sacred oral traditions about their ancestors, histories, and territories (Supreme Court Judgement, 1997). The Wet'suwet'en each have a "kungax," which is a spiritual song or dance or performance that ties them to their land. Both of these were entered as evidence on behalf of the appellants. The most significant evidence of a spiritual connection between the houses and their territory was a feast hall where the Gitksan and Wet'suwet'en people tell and retell their stories and identify their territories to remind themselves of the sacred connection they have with their lands. The feast has a ceremonial purpose but is also used for making important decisions.

Although blockchain technology has popularised this method, it has long been practiced through oral tradition. Due to this, praise poems are considered a trusted means of communicating and archiving ancestral heritage. It can even be used for genealogical research to compile a family tree. As Duranti (1994) argues, narrating oral history while sitting beyond the fire or at the feast, along with displaying crests and performing songs and family praises, confirms the people's official history. In this scenario, the process is a block, and witnesses are chains. Corroboration is used to authenticate oral history.

According to Lekgwathi (2014), other means of authenticating oral history when used as a method include questioning the informant's identity and their agendas (both public and hidden) when giving their accounts. Some may give accounts so that they can benefit from them; for example, a person who gives an account about an issue that will favour them, such as later using the information to claim land or chieftainship. In this regard, the informant's point of view of the event being described and how this has affected the way in which they are describing it should be probed so that authentic information is collected. Otherwise, if not properly probed, we can have one story with two different versions, as is the case with the story of the origin of the Malebogo nation on the north-western side of Polokwane in the Limpopo province of South Africa. Indeed, the story of the Bahananwa breaking away from Botswana, crossing the Limpopo River, and settling in the Blouberg has different versions. Although there are two versions, both acknowledge that Bahananwa broke away from Bahurutse in Botswana. The versions also acknowledge the naming of Bahananwa (those who refused to be ruled by King Malete) and the surname Lebogo (meaning a hand, but figuratively meaning such a nation would be an extension of the Bahurutse) (Setumu, 2019).

Perhaps a perfect example cited in Ngoepe (2020b) is the story about the origin of the name GaRankuwa, a township about 40 kilometres outside Pretoria.

> One oral narrative is that Garankuwa was named after a Bakgatla headman, Rankuwa Boikhutso. Rankuwa means 'we are taken'. When they arrived in the area, which was infertile and unsuited for farming, they named it Ga-Rankuwa, which means 'We are not taken'. Another explanation for the name of the township is that it was named after a prominent follower of Chief Mamogale named RraNkuwa (Father Nkuwa or Mr. Nkuwa), and his lands were often referred to as Ga-Rankuwa, or 'at Mr. Nkuwa's'. The third meaning of the name came from the fact that the previous owner of the land had many sheep and was known as the "father of sheep" (Rra-nku). "Ga-Ranku" refers to the place of the father of sheep. In this regard, it is difficult to confirm the correct version. Different versions of stories are most common in chieftainship squabbles. Therefore, it is essential that techniques from other fields of studies, such as archival science, be used to authenticate oral history. Archival science is relevant as the products of oral history are lodged in the archive repositories.

Many of the same issues arise when using written records, as written sources can also contain personal or social biases because they occur in a social context. It is worth noting that even written records can result in two non-identical originals. Ngoepe and Netshakhuma (2018) provide an example of such records, which are two non-identical copies of the Freedom Charter created at a meeting attended by approximately 3,000 delegates, which was broken up by police on the second day, despite the fact that the charter had been read in full but had not been signed by then. Because copies of the Freedom Charter were later circulated underground for signatures, the order of the signatories in the two existing documents differs. As a result, the copy at the National Archives of South Africa and the copy at the Liliesleaf Museum are not identical, particularly in the order of the signatories, despite the fact that the content is the same. In some cases, some signatories signed only one copy. However, attendees at the meeting were later able to confirm the authenticity of the two copies.

Individuals, communities, and nations can express their identities through the names of their villages, totems, personal names, and praise poems, but these identities must be observed and validated by others.

Murals

In Chapter One, murals were construed as extended archives. In this regard, it was stated that the original copy could be found in an archive repository. According to Ngoepe and Mosako (2022), this is done to bring archives to the people. Such an initiative is a worthwhile endeavour that aims to broaden society's knowledge base. As a result, extended archives in the form of murals offer more pros than cons. While the murals provide historical information and are useful to the public, they do have limitations. Wear and tear is usually an issue, as in the case of the mural depictions at Lctlamorcng Dam, where parts of the depictions are peeled off and indirectly misrepresent the original depictions. However, it should be noted that the original records are still kept at the archives, and the 'extended archive' is only temporary. Furthermore, some of the depicted portraits have been defaced, resulting in distorted representations of the original depictions by the commissioned artists. The custodians of the walls on which the murals are depicted classify such distortions as vandalism. However, the distortions could also be the result of protests against the murals' depictions. To validate extended archives, archivists or

76 *Authentication of indigenous archives*

muralists can capture metadata with fields describing the location of the original record, and identity metadata (the name of the muralist who painted the wall, as well as date and time), the record description, and other necessary fields. Such murals can also be digitised and displayed on the websites of archival repositories. It should also be noted that commissioned murals are frequently altered. This was the case with murals in Durban, which changed from KwaZulu-Natal kings to mayors of the City of eThekwini. Such modifications should also be documented, along with the coordinates of the location where they are painted.

Rock art paintings

Rock art paintings are some of the memories that have been conceptualised as indigenous archives. They have an embedded structure aimed at communicating information. For them to be authenticated, we need to discover such a structure. Furthermore, like murals, rock art paintings can also be assigned metadata. Most of these paintings are in the mountains. To be identified as an archival diplomatic, an entity must have stable content and fixed form and be affixed to a stable medium or physical carrier, which rock art paintings do. It is a timeless tradition of creating and preserving information. As reflected in Figure 1.1 in Chapter One, some of these rock art paintings are fading due to rain. Most of the rock art paintings that have been discovered have been digitised. One such project is The African Rock Art Digital Archive (sarada.co.za), which contains a comprehensive catalogue of rock art paintings, not only in South Africa but also other African countries. This is a way of preserving and keeping a surrogate in the digital format. Such formats can be used to generate funds, especially if the picture is used in a publication or other means. While we encourage ethnography researchers and tourists to visit the sites, perhaps digitisation can also help to raise awareness of the existence of such paintings and catalogues shared with tourism entities. Where they are fenced, we noted that the park owners wrote disclaimers on the boards for visitors such as:

> Treat the rock art as you would a picture in your house or in a gallery. Do not place graffiti on a rock art site as it is often

impossible to remove. Do not walk or touch the rocks that bear images, do not scratch, or paint them.

These illegal practices obscure and damage the art. Such notices educate the public about the importance of rock art paintings. Rock art is important because it demonstrates that people in the past had ideas as sophisticated and understanding as we do today, but they cannot be replaced. It is a reminder of how people in the past understood relationships between themselves and their natural environment.

An individual with specific relevant expertise in rock art paintings can perform authentication. Where rock art paintings are vandalised, there should be some form of restriction of access to the sites without supervision. As it stands, rock art paintings such as the ones in Makgabeng can be accessed by anybody at any time without supervision.

Rock art paintings have stable content as the data and the message they convey are unchanged and unchangeable, meaning that data cannot be overwritten, altered, deleted, or added to. As is the case with archival diplomatics, a declaration made by a rock art painting expert can also be used to authenticate such records.

Laws

Several South African and Zimbabwean laws, including the National Archives and Records Service Act of South Africa (Act No. 43 of 1996), the Traditional Leadership and Governance Framework Act of South Africa (Act No. 41 of 2003), the National Heritage Resources Act of South Africa (Act No. 25 of 1999), the National Heritage Council Act of South Africa (Act No. 11 of 1999), as well as the Copyright and Neighbouring Rights Act of Zimbabwe (Act No. 26 of 2004) and the Traditional Leaders Act of Zimbabwe (Act No. 29 of 2001), were examined to determine whether provision is made for conceptualised indigenous archives as records.

While the Traditional Leadership and Governance Framework Act recognises traditional communities, it does not mention oral history as evidence, despite the fact that the communities it serves are based on oral memory. The law seeks to restore the integrity and legitimacy of the traditional leadership institution in accordance with customary law and practices, but it makes no mention of this institution's source of evidence or the evidence itself, which is oral memory. It is mostly for show and only exists for ceremonial purposes. It could be because it is based on Roman law while dealing with indigenous issues. This is not unique to South Africa; according to Walkem (2005), the introduction of indigenous oral traditions as evidence in court is a political contingent in Canada because these laws have yet to flow back onto the land and be invigorated in law.

Even in South Africa, customary marriage law does not mention oral memory as evidence. This is exacerbated by the fact that the primary archival legislation, the National Archives and Records Service of South Africa Act, is devoid of references to oral history. The only provision may be in the (mis)interpretation of section 3(d), which indicates the function to collect non-public records of enduring value and national significance that cannot be more appropriately preserved by another institution, with due regard for the need to document aspects of the nation's experience that have previously been neglected by archives repositories. It should be noted, however, that no mention of oral history or any identified indigenous archive is made. The key words are 'non-public record' and 'significant value,' but the White Paper on Arts and Culture specifies oral memory by outlining government policy for the promotion, protection, creation, and funding of South African arts, including written and oral literature, culture, heritage, and associated practitioners. In addition, the National Heritage Council Act (Act No. 11 of 1999) classifies oral history and indigenous knowledge systems are classified as part of living heritage without specifying what they entail. This is also the case with the National Heritage Resources Act, which classifies oral history as living heritage, as it states in its preamble that

> our heritage celebrates our achievements and contributes to redressing past inequities. It educates, it deepens our understanding of society and encourages us to empathise with the experience of others. It facilitates healing and material and symbolic restitution, and it promotes new and previously neglected research into our rich oral traditions and customs.

Furthermore, in terms of section 2(ii)b of the National Heritage Council Act (Act No. 11 of 1999), rock art, being any form of painting, engraving or other graphic representation on a fixed rock surface or loose rock or stone, which was executed by human agency and which is older than 100 years, including any area within 10 m of such representation

are considered national estate and fall within the sphere of operations of heritage resources authorities. Reference is also made to the National Archives and Records Service of South Africa in the National Heritage Council Act. It is worth noting that the legislation in Zimbabwe is silent on indigenous archives. While the Traditional Leaders Act of Zimbabwe (Act No. 29 of 2001) only touches on the political side, the Copyright and Neighbouring Rights Act of Zimbabwe (Act No. 26 of 2004) does mention copyright about folklore (this is discussed in Chapter Four).

Conclusion

In general, validation of oral tradition is through trust, corroboration, and witnesses. An attempt was made by the UN Declaration on the Rights of Indigenous Peoples between 9 and 11 February 2005, in support of the Global Research Alliance and the World Bank, the Swiss Development Corporation, and the Department of Science and Technology of the government of South Africa to bring together scientists, traditional healers, and decision and policy makers to discuss how to jointly approach the validation of indigenous knowledge (Gorjestani, 2005). However, the emphasis was more on recognition, sharing, and protection of traditional medicine. Perhaps, a similar workshop is needed for indigenous archives.

It is apparent that some elements of diplomatic and blockchain can be used to authenticate oral history, as the preservation of oral memory, like digital memory, depends on proactive effort to migrate from one carrier to another. We need to know what act or fact is being recorded in order to attest to its authenticity for the purposes of preservation and future reference. As a result, indigenous archives can be referred to as records. The indigenous archive tradition corresponded to the concept expressed by the definition provided by archival theory. Indigenous archives should be viewed as a supplement, not an exclusive source, in the project of documenting history for the previously marginalised. In all the indigenous archives discussed, the information is stored and deemed worthy of retention by its creator for its own future reference.

References

Duranti, L. (1994). The records: where archival universality resides. *Archival Issues*, 19(2): 83–94.
Duranti, L. (2009). From digital diplomatics to digital records forensics. *Archivaria*, (68):39–66.
Gorjestani, N. (2005). Validation of indigenous knowledge. *International Workshop Benoni, South Africa*, 9–11 February 2005. Available at: http://web.worldbank.org/archive/website01219/WEB/IMAGES/GORJESTA.PDF (Accessed 1 February 2023).
Harris, V. (1997). *Exploring archives: an introduction to archival ideas and practice in South Africa*. 1st ed. Pretoria: National Archives of South Africa.
Harris, V. (2000). *Exploring archives: an introduction to archival ideas and practice in South Africa*. 2nd ed. Pretoria: National Archives of South Africa.
Hatang, S. (2000). Converting orality to material custody: is it a noble act of liberation or is it an act of incarceration? *ESRABICA Journal*, 19: 22–30.
Lekgwathi, S.P. (2014). *Oral history and historical research in South Africa: some theoretical issues.* Paper presented at the Annual Conference of the South African Society of Archivists, Nelspruit, 9–11 July.
Lowry, J. (n.d.). The inverted archive: thresholds, authenticity and the demos.
Macdonald, W. (1995). *Archival theory and oral history documents.* MA dissertation, Vancouver, University of British Columbia.
Moloto, L. (2021). Prologue: Leokama Moloto's royal welcome to Mošate. In T. Setumu. *History of Batlhaloga of Moloto Kingdom*. Polokwane: Mak Herp.
Ngoepe, M. (2012). *Fostering a framework to embed the records management function into the auditing process in the South African public sector.* PhD thesis, Pretoria: University of South Africa.
Ngoepe, M. (2020a). Whose truth is true? The use of archival principles to authenticate oral history. In P. Ngulube (Ed.), *Handbook of research on connecting research methods for information science*, Hershey: IGI Global, 307–319.
Ngoepe, M. (2020b). *Stir the dust: memoirs of a Comrades champion, Ludwick Mamabolo*. Polokwane: Mak Herp.

Ngoepe, M. (2022). Neither prelegal nor nonlegal: oral memory in troubled times. *HTS Teologiese Studies/Theological Studies*, 78(3): 6.

Ngoepe, M. and Mosako, R.D. (2022). Walls have ears and eyes: taking 'extended archives' to the people through murals. *Journal of Archival Organization*, volume ahead of print.

Ngoepe, M., Mukwevho, J. and Mosweu, O. (2022). Authenticating digital records to support auditing process. In M. Ngoepe (Ed.). Managing digital records in Africa. London: Routledge, pp. 71–86.

Ngoepe, M. and Netshakhuma, S. (2018). Archives in the trenches: repatriation of African National Congress liberation archives in diaspora to South Africa. *Archival Science*, 18: 51–71.

Ngoepe, M. and Ngulube, P. (2014). Eternal memory or holy amnesia? Preservation of, and access to, records and archives of African Independent churches in South Africa. *ESRABICA Journal*, 33: 36–45.

Pearce-Moses, R, (2019). InterPARES Trust terminology. In L. Duranti and C. Rogers (Eds.), *Trusting records in the cloud*, London: Facet Publishing, 267–286.

Setumu, T. (2010). *Communal identity creation among the Makgabeng rural people in Limpopo Province*. PhD thesis, University of Limpopo, Turfloop.

Setumu, T. (2019). Setlogo sa Bahananwa. In M. Ngoepe and N. Marutha (Eds.), *Bohwa bjarena*, Pretoria: University of South Africa, 24–37.

Stancic, H., Ngoepe, M. and Mukwevho, J. (2019). Authentication. In L. Duranti and C. Rogers (Eds.), *Trusting records in the cloud*. London: Facet Publishing, 135–154.

Supreme Court Judgement. (1997). Delgamuukw v. British Columbia, 11 December. Available at: https://scc-csc.lexum.com/scc-csc/scc-csc/en/item/1569/index.do (Accessed 12 August 2022).

Tough, A.G. (2012). Oral culture, written records and understanding the twentieth-century colonial archive: the significance of understanding from within. *Archival Science*, 12: 245–265.

Turner, D. (2012). Oral documents in concept and in situ, part I: Grounding an exploration of orality and information behavior. *The Journal of Documentation*, 68(6): 852–863. doi:10.1108/00220411211277073

Walkem, A.A. (2005). *Water to the land: re-cognize-ing Indigenous oral traditions and the law embodied within them*. Master of Law, Vancouver, University of British Columbia.

Yeo, G. (2019). *Why study histories of records and archives?* Paper presented at AERI Conference, Liverpool, 8–12 July.

4 Ownership, copyright, and 'copyleft' of indigenous archives

Introduction

Indigenous archives such as oral history, rock art paintings, and murals are open to abuse because ownership of such archives is not clear. Furthermore, they are often excluded from heritage, archival, and copyright legislation. Hence, a study by Ngoepe (2020) recommended that future research directions should look at interrogating the issues of ownership, copyleft, and copyright of oral history and other types of indigenous archives with the view to developing guidelines for their protection. This is because such archives are often exploited by outsiders without the benefits of communities that are the custodians of such knowledge. A close example but not related is when Livingstone is credited with discovering *Mosi-oa-Tunya* (the smoke that thunders), which is popularly known as the Victoria Falls. Instead of being credited with popularising the Falls, he is credited with discovering it, as if no one had gone there before him and no one has showed it to him. This can also happen with the identified indigenous archives. Therefore, it is necessary to establish how these archives are copyrighted or copylefted and to determine their ownership.

Saurombe (2013) views knowledge from these archives as a significant resource that can contribute to the increased efficiency, effectiveness, and sustainability of the development process on the African continent. He propagates for the development of indigenous knowledge system policies to realise the contribution of indigenous archives to the grand societal problems. Saurombe (2013) is of the view that policies will lead to the protection of indigenous knowledge, and this may propel the continent to

DOI: 10.4324/9781003277989-5

emerge as a key player in the global knowledge-based economy. Otherwise, if not protected, the owners of these archives may end up being gate-crashers to the party of their knowledge, while those who are outsiders become the gatekeepers, preventing the owners from accessing it, as is the case currently with some of the sites. It is therefore necessary that measures be put in place to safeguard indigenous archives. This chapter interrogates issues relating to ownership, copyleft, and copyright of indigenous archives such as oral memory, rock art paintings, and murals. This is done through analysing archival and heritage legislation and policies. Saurombe (2013) calls for mechanisms to ensure collaboration between those in possession of these archives and the communities of government, civil society, and academia to create a large reservoir of intellectual capital. This should in turn be accompanied by an equitable legal dispensation to protect indigenous knowledge that is built on respect for human dignity and African cultural values (Saurombe, 2013).

Ownership

In this section, we look at ownership of land during the precolonial and colonial periods, as well as its impact on indigenous archives due to the European notions of ownership that impinge on pre-existing understandings. This is necessary as colonisers carved up land using documents.

Land resources

In precolonial times, the indigenous peoples of South Africa had abundant land, with farming and herding being the predominant economic activities. African communities organised their societies under political rulers from macro to micro levels in their various areas. At the macro level, nations were organised under the ruler, which is the king, with the next layer of political rulership being that of headmen, who ruled over smaller sections of the kingdom under the king. The last unit of the society was the family. These societies were built around people, in which allegiance to leadership was paramount. In this regard, Setumu (2021) contends that communities were organised and identified themselves into units of families, clans, villages, and politics with varying sizes and powers. The need to belong together for common destiny was important because as a collective, people were stronger as they held one another's hands in any situation, be it political, economic, cultural, or otherwise. In this context, human beings were important, while during colonialism, material resources were sought after. The African socio-political systems were flexible, as manifested in the economic element of ownership of land and resources on it (Setumu, 2021). It should be noted that there were small families that survived several onslaughts such as 'Mfecane' by lying low in areas that were not accessible by passers-by. Ngoepe and Setumu (2022) identify such families around the Makgabeng Mountains as Phukubje, Setumu, Masekwa, and Ngoepe.

Unlike Eurocentric approaches, African communities did not see land and its resources as pieces of commodities which should be divided and owned privately. As Du Plessis (2006) would attest, the concept of ownership was limited in precolonial South Africa and more often embedded in status relationships. Put differently, African indigenous law in property was more concerned with people's obligations towards one another in respect of property than with the rights of people in property. Setumu (2021) emphasises that African communities understood that land and its resources should be owned, used, and shared communally among all the people. In this regard, the relationships between people were more important than an individual's ability to assert his or her interest in property against the world. Interestingly, land resources were even shared between communities of different units, in which there were no hard, fenced borders with free movement among different political communities where people identified themselves through their kings, clans, and family praises. Entitlements to property were more in the form of obligations resulting from family relationships than a means to exclude people from the use of certain property (Du Plessis, 2006). This way, property was seen in precolonial Africa as embedded in social relationships rather than giving rise to an individual's exclusive claim over it as private property.

Colonial government disrupted the whole system and deprived people of their land through various means of aggression, treachery, as well as enforced pieces of legislation. Some of these pieces of legislation that come to mind are the 1913 Land Act and 1927 Bantu Administration Act. Of interest is that out of

Afrocentric arrangement, communities were arranged socially rather than geographically. Geographic and physical landmarks as boundaries were less important because households, families, and clans were the ones that counted as building blocks of communities. The demarcation of land created problems and dislocated families, hence most lost their way of doing things, including family praises and ancestral land. The colonisers carved up land using written documents. This resulted in ownership of land through archival documents such as title deeds.

While African ownership of land was communal, people paid allegiance to the king who was also the custodian of heritage. However, as indicated earlier regarding land, ownership of indigenous archives was also classified from macro to micro levels, that is, from the king, to headmen to clans and families. Indigenous archives were not given space and freedom to grow; as a result, it had limited scope to develop at its own pace and based on its own principles. This was due to a number of factors such as displacement of families and deposing of kings by those who supported colonial government. This resulted in indigenous archives being externalised through commercialisation in some instances. In the process, in the case of rock art sites, those who now own the areas because they purchased the land, are now making people pay to view these sites. This takes us back to the notion of gate-crashers becoming gatekeepers and those who previously owned the land becoming gate-crashers. It should be noted that this is not limited to rock art paintings, as some coastal areas are also private and not accessible by ordinary citizens. In the current dispensation, local government authorities are supposed to be the custodians of heritage, including the rock art paintings. This is not the case in many municipalities, especially in rural areas, as these municipalities do not have heritage practitioners. For example, Blouberg Local Municipality, where the rock art paintings of Makgabeng are situated, has only one heritage practitioner who is not supported for preservation of such heritage. The rock art paintings are not easily accessible by car, as there is no road. The inaccessibility of such rock art paintings is considered as one way of ensuring their protection and preservation, as highlighted in an interview with one of the heritage consultants. However, as Matshotshwane and Ngoepe (2022) would ask why take a golden bulb and wrap it in a dark cloth. Indeed, we cannot light a lamp and cover it with a bowl. We should instead place it on a stand so that it gives light to everyone in the house. In the context of indigenous archives, these should be accessible so they also contribute to solving grand societal challenges.

Indigenous archives

Several authors, such as Ngoepe and Netshakhuma (2018), Ngoepe (2020; 2022), and Saurombe (2013), to mention just a few, have written about the ownership of indigenous archives. However, the emphasis by Saurombe (2013) was more on indigenous knowledge systems (IKS) in its entity, while Ngoepe (2020; 2022) was specific about oral history. Saurombe (2013) went further to identify policy provisions on indigenous knowledge systems in several countries in the Southern African Development Community (SADC) region. He identifies countries such as South Africa, Malawi, Namibia, and Seychelles as progressing in terms of regularising IKS. For example, in Seychelles, the protection of IKS is the responsibility of the Ministry of the Arts, Culture and Sports, with the National Heritage Research Section, under this Ministry, given the mandate through a unit called the Oral Tradition and Anthropology to look after the intangible aspects of the country's culture, which includes knowledge systems such as oral history. In this regard, the Ministry conducts research and documents everything to do with the country's tradition. Furthermore, the other unit within the Ministry, the Cultural Property Unit, is responsible for safeguarding traditional knowledge in all its aspects, making sure that nothing from Seychelles is taken as the property of another country (Saurombe, 2013).

While Botswana has acknowledged the importance of IKS, it has yet to develop the policies and regulations to protect this treasure. The same can be said about Zimbabwe. On the other hand, South Africa and Namibia have made strides in this field. For example, in Namibia, Vision 2030 addresses issues of IKS. The country has established the Traditional Healers Association of Namibia to deal with herbal medicine practices and applications. In addition, the National Culture and Heritage Council of Namibia deals with IKS and folklore.

In South Africa, as in other developing countries, there is no legal redress that addresses either the protection or commercialisation of traditional knowledge and no legal instruments that deal with collective ownership of traditional knowledge or benefit traditional knowledge holders. Instead, the South African government, through the Ministry of Science and Technology, has developed a policy framework for the protection of indigenous knowledge systems. When it comes to indigenous archives within IKS, even pieces of legislation such as the National Archives and Records Service Act (Act No. 43 of 1996) are silent. The policy framework for the protection of indigenous knowledge makes several recommendations, such as:

> Where there is an invention emanating from the application of indigenous knowledge, a disclosure of the origin of indigenous resources should be made, as well as prior informed concern of the people from which the knowledge is derived, benefit-sharing agreements, and co-ownership of the patent.

Patents are used as an intellectual property tool to protect indigenous knowledge in this regard because the scope for ownership and commercial sharing is broad. According to the policy framework, the only significant shortcoming is the limited time frame, which does not allow for perpetual benefits to knowledge holders. The policy recognises that, due to intellectual property limitations, some users are hijacking indigenous knowledge under the guise of intellectual property by registering ownership without benefiting local people. One might wonder who owns rock art paintings like those found on the Makgabeng plateau and elsewhere. These rock art paintings benefit only a few locals who serve as tour guides for visitors.

Saurombe (2013) believes that contractual agreements can be used to protect indigenous knowledge, as has occurred on several occasions in South Africa, New Zealand, and Australia. This may ensure that the locals benefit from such knowledge. The policy framework for indigenous knowledge systems also allows folklore owners to licence their work to third parties for exploitation and then receive royalties on agreed-upon terms. A classic example is the saga surrounding the ownership of the Xhosa tribe's folklore song Mbube. African Independent Churches, such as the Zion Christian Church (ZCC), have not been immune to the exploitation of traditional church songs, with members and non-members alike frequently using church songs in their music, the most popular of which is "mpogo." Lebeloane and Madise (n.d.) define "mpogo" as a ritual prayer song sung in the ZCC to pray for peace and a peaceful resolution of problems. Engenas Lekganyane, the church's founder, wrote the song in the early 1900s. Since the ZCC relies heavily on oral history as a means of communication, most early church activities were not documented and were instead passed down through word of mouth. Many musicians have made a fortune from the song "mpogo" without paying royalties to the church.

It should be noted that the issue of ownership extends to written records and is not limited to only indigenous archives. Ngoepe (2020), for example, provides a report on the case of Steve Biko's autopsy:

> In December 2014, the High Court in Johannesburg granted an interdict on the sale of Steve Biko's autopsy report from 1977, which contains certificates from pathologists, a certificate in terms of the Criminal Procedure Act, and a 43-page postmortem report. This report was given to Maureen Steele, the personal secretary of Dr. Jonathan Gluckman, the pathologist appointed by the Biko family. Dr. Gluckman was very concerned about the safety of such documents as his offices had been bugged and he had received numerous death threats. He therefore asked Mrs Steele to keep the copies of such documents. Steele passed away in 2014, and the documents went to her children, who did not want them. It was unknown if the children gave them or sold them to Westgate Walding, which was auctioning the documents when interdicted by the Steve Biko Foundation, which believes the documents belong to the Biko family.

Even though it is a private matter, the issue of ownership arises in this account. To make matters more complicated, Ngoepe (2020) reports that the Steele siblings' attorney argued that the document was simply a copy of the original report, which had been in the public domain for 37 years. The same thing can happen with a written record as with oral history, resulting in two different versions. In this case, two copies are kept by two different people. The same thing can happen to oral history if more than one person knows a story, folktale, family praise, songs, or any other form of oral memory. According to Ngoepe (2020), the advantage of oral memory is that the storyteller retains control over his story even after it has been narrated. Such a custodian can still narrate the story to others at his own pace, resulting in many copies that are not identical because audience members can (re)narrate the same story in slightly different ways (Ngoepe, 2022).

Copyright

Due to the fluid nature of indigenous archives, the application of intellectual property and copyright law can be broader and more difficult to navigate issue. Difficult questions arise regarding which laws apply to these archives and the responsibilities of those who create and own this information. Copyright is the exclusive and assignable legal right granted to the originator to print, publish, perform, film, or record literary, artistic, or musical material for a set number of years. As stated previously, indigenous archives, by definition, lack formal standards governing how they can be stored. Only literary works, musical works, artistic works, cinematograph film works, sound recordings, broadcasts, programme-carrying signals, published editions, and computer programs are protected under South Africa's Copyright Act. A work must be written down, recorded, or otherwise reduced to material form in order to be eligible for copyright. It excludes indigenous archives and any other publicly available information. This includes written records. Ngoepe (2021), for example, reports that the South African History Archives (SAHA) has created an archive of material made available to the public under the Promotion of Access to Information Act (Act No. 2 of 2000). SAHA scans and digitises materials obtained primarily from South Africa's National Archives and Records Services. One commentator argued that because these records are in the public domain, they are exempt from copyright laws. The provenance of the records is ensured through cataloguing and cross-referencing to the originals held by the South African National Archives and Records Services.

Only the expression of an idea is protected by copyright. If a community collectively owns the copyright, there is no such thing as a "copyright owner's" limited lifespan. To protect a local community's copyright, defensive protection, unfair competition, and confidential information protection may be used. The holders would grant the right to make reproductions through licensing and thus would be able to collect royalties indefinitely. Communities could form collecting societies or trusts to manage their collective rights and, as a result, negotiate and receive royalties for sharing.

While South African copyright laws are silent on indigenous archives, the South African Heritage Resource Agency has been given authority to protect national heritage sites. It should be noted, however, that most of the rock art painting sites have not been declared as heritage sites.

Of interest is that the Copyright and Neighbouring Rights Act of Zimbabwe (Act No. 26 of 2004) makes provision for copyright of folklore. This is an oral tradition that has been exploited for commercial gains. Part VIII of the Act is dedicated to the work of folklore. In this regard, it covers rights, restrictions, freedom, and licensing of folklore. Folklore is defined by the Act as meaning a literary, musical, or artistic work, whether or not it is recorded, of which (a) no person can claim to be the author; and (b) the form or content is embodied in the traditions peculiar to one or more communities in Zimbabwe; and includes:

(i) folk tales, folk poetry, and traditional riddles
(ii) folk songs and instrumental folk music
(iii) folk dances, plays and artistic forms of ritual
(iv) productions of folk art, in particular drawings, paintings, sculptures, pottery, woodwork, metalwork, jewellery, baskets, and costumes.

Three entities are identified in the Act as authorities for folklore, that is "appropriate local authority" (a local authority to which rights in relation to a work of folklore have been reserved), "community" (a community of persons who have inhabited Zimbabwe continuously since before 1890 and whose members share the same language or dialect or the same cultural values, traditions, or customs), and "public institution" (any association or body, whether corporate or unincorporated, established by or under an enactment, which is engaged in the promotion, preservation, or development of works of folklore, and includes a museum, library, art gallery, arts foundation, or arts group). The Act prohibits the reproduction, publishing, importing, performing, and broadcasting of folklores without the permission of the Minister or owners of the folklores. However, the Minister in charge may, by notice in the Gazette, reserve to the President the exclusive right to authorise the doing of any one or more of the above (reproduction, publishing, importing, performing, and broadcasting) in relation to a work of folklore whose form or content is embodied in the traditions of all communities within Zimbabwe. Local authority can also be grated such exclusive rights.

- A performance of a work of folklore to which Part VIII applies may be recorded for the purpose of including it in an archive which is not maintained for commercial purposes, and such a recording shall not be regarded as infringing the performer's right.

Copyleft

While indigenous archives are not protected by copyright, Ngoepe (2020) believes that oral memory, like open-source software, may allow stories to be 'copylefted.' Copyleft is thought to have originated with the work of MIT computer expert Richard Stallman (Söderberg, 2002). Copyleft is founded on the concept of copyright, without which it would be impossible to exist. Copyleft is defined by Ngoepe (2015, p. 191) as a "legal arrangement that allows software or artistic work to be freely used, modified, and distributed on the condition that anything derived from it is subject to the same conditions." In this regard, the product is made free in the sense that it is 'uncopyrighted' and thus 'copylefted' during the process (Ngoepe, 2015, p. 191). The practice of copyleft has been in existence in indigenous communities unconsciously since time immemorial. This can also be applied to oral memory and rock art paintings. Copyleft is an agreement that allows software or artistic work to be freely used, modified, and distributed on the condition that anything derived from it is subject to the same conditions. Copyleft is a general method for making a programme (or other work) free (in the sense of freedom, not "zero price") and requiring all modified and extended versions to be free as well. The most straightforward way to make a programme free software is to place it in the public domain, unprotected. While this can be extended to indigenous archives, Maluleka and Ngoepe (2018) lament the fact that communities are missing out on a chance to make a living because oral tradition is freely available.

The Copyright and Neighbouring Rights Act of Zimbabwe covers copyleft. The Act makes provision for freedom to do certain things in relation to reserved works of folklore without infringing on the copyright of a work. This may be done in relation to a reserved work of folklore without a licence granted. Exemption is made for a gain (i) where the right to do the thing has been reserved to the President, the person is a citizen of Zimbabwe and he does the thing for his personal gain or for the gain of other persons who are citizens of Zimbabwe; or (ii) where the right to do the thing has been reserved to a community, the person is a member of that community and he does the thing for his personal gain or for the gain of other persons who are members of that community. Furthermore, any person may use a reserved work of folklore to create an original work. In South Africa, for example, many books have been written and television series created based on folklore. Yet, there is no legislation addressing the issue. In Zimbabwe, the Minister or the appropriate local authority concerned may grant a written licence to any person or class of persons authorising him or them, as the case may be, to do anything in relation to a reserved work of folklore, where the right to do that thing has been reserved for the appropriate local authority.

Conclusion

This chapter interrogated issues concerning indigenous archives' ownership, copyright, and copyleft. This was accomplished by reviewing identified indigenous archives such as oral history, murals, and rock art paintings. It is apparent that establishing indigenous archive ownership is essential. If such ownership is transferred to a cultural institution, such as an archive repository or a museum, through oral history recording, the originators should be acknowledged, and if any proceedings take place, they should share the profit through contractual agreements. Owners of indigenous archives are not easy to identify in the current moment, except where the rock art paintings form part of someone's property. It has been observed that where owners of indigenous archives are known, quite often they fall victim to ambiguous service agreements or individuals who register patents without involving the owners of such knowledge. While South African copyright, archival, and heritage laws clearly exclude indigenous archives from their provisions, the Zimbabwean copyright law does make provision for protection of folklore. As a result, heritage laws in South Africa and archival law in Zimbabwe should be revised to include copyright and ownership of indigenous archives. It is clear that copyleft is applicable to indigenous archives and has been practised unconsciously for a long time. In Zimbabwe, it is even included in copyright legislation. Archivists and heritage practitioners should be involved in developing guidelines for ownership, copyright, and copyleft of indigenous archives. Failure to do that will result in these archives continuing to be exploited. Indeed, there is a need to rethink how the indigenous archives can be copyrighted without violating its communal use vis-à-vis commercialisation.

References

Du Plessis, A. (2006). Land restitution through the lens of environmental law: some comments on the South African vista. *Potchefstroom Electronic Law Journal*, 9(1). Available at: www.ajol.info/index.php/pelj/article/view/43450 (Accessed 18 July 2022).

Lebeloane, L. and Madise, M. (n.d.). The relevance of oral history as a methodology of research in church history: the case of the Zion Christian Church. Available at: https://uir.unisa.ac.za/bitstream/handle/10500/4485/Lebeloane-Madise.pdf?sequence=1&isAllowed=y (Accessed 10 July 2022).

Maluleka, J.R. and Ngoepe, M. (2018). Accumulation of cultural capital: the acquisition of indigenous knowledge by traditional healers in the Limpopo Province of South Africa. *International Journal of Knowledge Management Studies*, 9(3): 278–292.

Matshotshwane, J. and Ngoepe, M. (2022). Golden bulb covered with a dark cloth: memories of undocumented athletes in South Africa. *ESARBICA Journal*, 41: 1–17.

Ngoepe, M. (2015). Deployment of open source electronic content management software in national government departments in South Africa. *Journal of Science & Technology Policy Management*, 6(3): 190–205.

Ngoepe, M. (2020). Whose truth is true? The use of archival principles to authenticate oral history. In P. Ngulube (Ed.), *Handbook of research on connecting research methods for information science*. Hershey: IGI Global, pp. 307–319.

Ngoepe, M. (2021). Balancing and reconciling the conflicting values of information access and personal data laws in South Africa. In D. Ocholla, N.D. Evans and J.J. Britz (Eds.), *Information knowledge and technology for development in Africa*, OAIS: Durbanville, pp. 71–84.

Ngoepe, M. (2022). Neither prelegal nor nonlegal: oral memory in troubled times. *HTS Teologiese Studies/Theological Studies*, 78(3): 6.

Ngoepe, M. and Netshakhuma, S. (2018). Archives in the trenches: repatriation of African National Congress liberation archives in diaspora to South Africa. *Archival Science*, 18(1): 51–71.

Ngoepe, M. and Setumu, T. (2022). *Setlaole our home: our heritage, history, and culture*. MARKHERP: Polokwane.

Republic of South Africa. (2008). Policy framework for the protection of indigenous traditional knowledge through intellectual property system and the intellectual property laws amendment bill. Available at: www.gov.za/sites/default/files/gcis_document/201409/31026552.pdf (Accessed 10 December 2021).

Saurombe, A. (2013). Towards a harmonised protection of indigenous knowledge systems (IKS) in the Southern African Development Community (SADC): one step at a time. *ESARBICA Journal*, 32: 24–36.

Setumu, T. (2021). *Moletji: history of Batlhaloga of Moloto Kingdom*. Polokwane: Mak Herp.

Söderberg, J. (2002). Copyleft vs. copyright: a Marxist critique. *First Monday*, 7(3). https://doi.org/10.5210/fm.v7i3.938

5 Decolonisation and (re)Africanisation in action
A case study of community memory practices

Introduction

In order to demonstrate how indigenous archives operate or can work in a postcolonial context, this chapter focuses on a case study where such archives have been created and preserved. The case study used is that of the memorialisation of the lesbian, gay, bisexual, transgender, and intersex (LGBTI) community at the Gay and Lesbian Memory in Action (GALA) Archive in South Africa, paying particular attention to how they have used oral history to achieve that. They are not only interested in preserving pre- and post-apartheid historical records but they are also involved in documenting contemporary post-apartheid challenges faced by the LGBTI community. Other case studies, such as the Avuxeni Community Museum in Zimbabwe and the Makgabeng Rock Art Community Project in South Africa, are highlighted and mentioned in passing. These case studies give the hope of a possibility that a colonial archive can be decolonised and, at the same time, community archives that speak to the indigeneity of African people can be created.

One of the methodologies used by the indigenous subalterns to document their stories, which is oral history, was emphasised as a convenient and the best approach. The oral history epistemology risks being confused with the discourse intended to unearth the ancient, long-forgotten past. In South Africa, oral history has been widely used in documenting those masculine testimonies of the liberation struggle that led to independence in 1994 when apartheid was dismantled. Despite a few pockets of oral history programmes conducted by community and university

DOI: 10.4324/9781003277989-6

archives that target contemporary socio-political and economic challenges, there is still a gnawing gap in that aspect. However, GALA is an exception. Not only is it interested in the preservation of pre-apartheid historical records but it is also involved in the documentation of contemporary post-apartheid challenges faced by LGBTI people. Therefore, the purpose of this chapter is to critically analyse these oral history programmes at GALA, which have an emphasis on contemporary challenges, and to give an overview of the whole archival project at the institution and how it contributes to the archive that caters for everyone. One such programme is '#FeesMustFall,' which documents the experiences of tertiary queer and feminist students involved in the recent university student protests in South Africa.

Unpacking the philosophy behind community archives

Community archives come to the fore, mainly in addressing historical omissions, silences, absences, and, sometimes, archival debates, and putting to scrutiny the official national archive, which is usually prone to racism, tribalism, and exclusion. Flinn and Stevens (2009, p. 6) state that "community archives are motivated and prompted to act by the (real or perceived) failure of mainstream heritage organisations to collect, preserve, and make accessible collections and histories that properly reflect and accurately represent the stories of all society." Sheffield (2017, p. 351) describes the concept of community archives as

> the collections of local history museums, historical societies, ethno-cultural collections, religious and spiritual archives, resource centres, and sports and leisure clubs, as well as a growing number of activist archives that preserve materials related to social justice struggles for human rights.

Tribbett, Vo Dang, Yun and Zavala (2020, p. 7) designate community archives as

> any organisation that provides a platform outside of mainstream repositories for marginalised people to gain power over stories about their past. In their purest form, they employ a bottom-up approach to the creation, identification, preservation, and

dissemination of history. This directly challenges traditional archival practice, which privileges the expertise of library and archival professionals to serve as gatekeepers of historical records.

These community archives function as a counter-narrative to the marginalisation of any specific group in the production of authoritative forms of knowledge and thereby provide safe storage for the collection and its future use (Choudry & Vally, 2018, p. 6). For example, the lacunae in mainstream archives of women's stories of the African National Congress political party in South Africa of women who were involved in the liberation struggle has led to those narratives being counter archived by other parallel archives such as the Nelson Mandela Foundation (Netshakhuma, 2020). The motivation for documenting these women's stories is the fact that "existing historiography has from an early stage tended to dismiss or downplay the involvement of women in political struggle, for entering as 'mothers', or supportive of the role of men, or performing conventional female roles" (Suttner, 2007, p. 237).

Community archiving is more of a creative and innovative approach that experiments with pedagogical strategies and practices that lead to the construction, co-construction, documentation, recovery, and preservation of the "other" histories and ideas (Choudry & Vally, 2018, p. 2). Hence, the statement from Harrison (2021, p. 127) that community archives are fulfilling something otherwise unavailable in mainstream institutions. This quest of documenting the 'other' has led some scholars like Moran (2016, p. 4) to link community archiving with anarchism, being defined as "suspicious of the state and its institutions, have also wanted to protect their own historical writings and culture." Anarchist community archives are more "of the history of radical social struggles, especially in the local area" (Moran 2016, p. 7). In other words, community archives become centres of revolution, be it politically or socially. Community archiving is also linked with the sociology concept of community resilience, in which self-organisation and agency are the key pillars (Scott, 2014).

Because of the widespread use of digital tools, including Web 2.0, some of these community archives have taken to the online spaces, freeing themselves from the dominant archival practices that are based on the archive's fixity. Gibbons (2019, p. 2) labels online communal formations as the emergent community archives, which are "conceptualised as *outside* spaces, created for remembering and sharing identity and memory by utilising technology that appears suited to the purpose." Such an approach gives a chance for those who are not represented in the official archive to tell their stories because it is easier to open a Facebook account than to build a fixed archival building. In other words, the creation of these parallel online community archives could play a major role in the decolonisation and indigenisation of the colonial archive. It appears to already be happening on the African continent. Chirikure, Manyanga, Ndoro and Pwiti (2010, p. 30) explain that "the emergence of community participation and its derivatives has significantly shifted the pendulum of disciplinary practice in heritage management across the world." Chirikure et al. (2010, p. 38) continue to argue that "community participation is seen as an empowerment tool which could change the face of 'the western derived' heritage management practices."

Community archiving is giving archivists a learning platform to re-imagine the conventional archive and, in the process, allow the de-centering of the mainstream archive, thereby giving voices to the subaltern. Community archiving is more than engagement with the local people, as it is more about giving power to the communities to manage their heritage with minimal or zero interference from the state and its organs. In addition to that, Harrison (2021, p. 110) argues "that community archival practice is an important standpoint from which to critically reassess the capacity of institutional archives to create a more conscious and complete history through broader collecting." Community archiving by African communities also lends itself to Africanisation concepts which promote its knowledge systems. This is so because of the fact that if Africans continue to worry about changing the colonial archive instead of propagating their indigenous knowledge systems, it means they are the victims of the whiteness discourse, which portrays itself as central to knowledge production and reception (GALA, 2016, p. 148).

Some of the examples of community archiving found in Zimbabwe and South Africa are those of the Tso-ro-tso San Development Trust, Gaza Trust, Bafokeng Digital Archive, Jewish Digital Archive, and Makgabeng Community Rock Art Project. All these projects are driven by the emphasis on promoting and documenting the identity of their constituencies. The Gaza Trust runs the Avuxeni Community Museum, which "seeks to safeguard the indigenous knowledge and heritage of the Tsonga people who live in and around the Great Limpopo Transfrontier Conservation Area" (Pikela, Thondhlana & Madlome, 2022, p. 159). In other words, like many community archives in the world, the Avuxeni Community Museum "is meant to restore the dignity of the Tsonga people following decades of colonial and postcolonial marginalisation." The goal of the project is to bring the rich and resilient Tsonga culture back to life and celebrate it (Pikela et al., 2022, p. 161).

The Makgabeng Community Heritage Archive was established in 2012 in the tourism office building of the Blouberg Local Municipality in Senwabarwana town, Limpopo province, South Africa. The archive was "to house various things, which include oral histories and traditions collected through the Oral Heritage project, an offshoot of the Makgabeng Community Rock Art Heritage project" (Namono, 2018, p. 270). This archive speaks to the ownership by the community as it tries to document their culture and traditions, especially the ones that involve initiation to manhood and womanhood for both boys and girls (Namono, 2018). The importance of community ownership, as per community heritage management discourse in this project, is emphasised by Katsetse and Namono (2019, p. 361), who observe that

> the involvement of local communities is a critical component of a preventive conservation approach. Therefore, local communities are important partners in efforts to conserve rock art, especially since some of them still use these rock art sites for ritual ceremonies.

Ngoepe and Setumu (2016), however, mention that the History Museum and the Wits School of Rock Art became extensively involved in the research and documentation of the rock art of the Makgabeng. The earlier 2002 project implemented by one of the authors in that area drew heavily on such research works, and to a large extent, it involved local communities who were exposed to the rock art paintings. According to one of the project managers, because the local communities were involved in these projects, they began to value and appreciate their heritage and the rock art paintings, which they came to fondly refer to as 'dikgaatwanetša

Makgabeng' (lizards of Makgabeng), because, to them, the paintings looked like lizards on rocks (Setumu, 2010).

Deployment of oral history in community archives

Oral history is becoming increasingly important in the emancipation of knowledge silos in order to accommodate previously marginalised voices. Bhebhe and Ngoepe (2022, p. 178) aver that "oral history is being extolled as a methodology that captures and accommodates the voices of the minority groups, the subaltern, the once oppressed or marginalized, and, mostly, the African people whose history is mainly in an oral form." Bhebhe (2017, p. 2) states that

> oral history is but an approach within the wider methodological practice of life history and life story… The life history method is employed primarily in cultural anthropology to provide a rich, full description of an individual's life… Most importantly, the method allows for the life to be situated in a socio-historical context.

National mainstream archival centres are also using oral history to decolonise their collections, as specifically observed at the National Archives of Zimbabwe by Bhebhe (2015, p. 51) when he states that the institution "continues to use oral history as a tool to fill in the perceived gaps in the historical narrative of the nation of Zimbabwe." Unfortunately, this oral archive at the National Archives of Zimbabwe is being underutilised compared to other types of records (Bhebhe & Khumalo, 2019).

Oral history can create historically confident communities, as proffered by Bhebhe (2016, p. 9) when he argues that it

> is a powerful tool that can bring confidence to those communities that feel despised and marginalised. All this can be achieved by giving room to the communities to tell their stories themselves without having 'the big brother' to dictate who, how, and what should be noted in an oral history programme. Oral history should not just end with oral testimonies stored in archival institutions. It should go beyond that, especially for those societies that once suffered trauma. It should heal, offer confidence,

and make the community realise that they are important, and they have a worthy story to tell.

Such a communal approach to oral history is bearing fruit for the marginalised communities in Zimbabwe, especially the indigenous San people in Tsholotsho and Plumtree. The notable example is that, through their Tso-ro-tso San Development Trust, the San community has managed to translate the Constitution of Zimbabwe into their language, and they are addressing the possible extinction of their language by partnering with the University of Zimbabwe's African Languages Research Institute (Bhebhe, 2016). Therefore, these subaltern communities, such as the San in Zimbabwe, are creatively using their oral history programmes to not only archive their stories, but also address the contemporary challenges they are facing.

Oral history has been associated with community resilience. Bhebhe (2019, p. 279) states that "the advantage of documenting all the stories of all the minority groups is that this would assist them in their respective communities to overcome challenges they face." Madsen (2015, p. 56) also outlines how oral history leads to community resilience by "increasing capacity, collective problem solving and action by community members and uncovering stories of the past that are used to support and strengthen a social narrative of how the community can respond to change and adversity." In other words, oral history is viewed as a powerful tool in fostering community resilience. Scott (2014, p. 38) argues that current literature about social-ecological resilience highlights the "importance of historical oral communication in storing and sharing memories that shape local culture and inform what and how livelihoods are pursued." Scott continues to argue that "these memories form the basis of Traditional Environmental Knowledge (TEK), which is most often learned and acquired through oral transmission and physical demonstration."

During South Africa's apartheid regime, the state purposefully avoided documenting black people's stories. However, thanks to oral history, those omissions were taken care of by the use of oral history methodology. Saleh (2017, p. 6) enlightens how oral history was used during apartheid to document the other by stating that "oral testimonies added to the depth and knowledge of various struggles and campaigns waged in opposition to apartheid." An example of this is the History Workshop at Wits University, which was formed in 1977 to promote scholarly research into the lives and communities of black people who have been largely ignored by the academy. Saleh (2017, p. 6) goes on to mention some of the institutions that have used oral history to document the marginalised, such as the Mayibuye Centre at the University of the Western Cape, the District Six Museum, the National Heritage and Cultural Studies Centre (NAHECS), which houses the ANC and other liberation movement archives at the University of Fort Hare, and the South African History Archive (SAHA).

Theorisation of Africanisation and decolonisation in the Gay and Lesbian Memory in Action

Chitando and Mateveke (2017, p. 124) state that "one of the most abiding accusations in the debate on homosexuality in Africa is that the whole enterprise is 'western' and that it lacks 'a true African flavour'." Scholars like Epprecht (2004) have asked questions about whether homosexuality is indigenous to Africa or introduced from outside the continent. Chitando and Mateveke (2017, p. 124) further note that there is now the emergence of scholars who are using African epistemologies such as Africanisation to Africanise homosexuality discourse. In fact, some scholars like Ibrahim (2015, p. 263) argue that

> much of Africa seems to be riding on a homophobic wave that is being billed as an African resistance to Western attempts to force homosexuality on Africa. However, this Africanisation of homophobia is based on false premises. Pre-colonial Africa entertained a diverse set of ways in which non-heterosexuality and non-heteronormativity were expressed and it was colonialism that introduced the now widespread religious and legal norms that policed sexuality and gender.

Kaunda (2013, p. 55) talks about same-sex relationships still commonly practiced by sangomas (traditional healers) in KwaZulu-Natal. Kaunda (2013, p. 55) further argues that "the practice of same sex relationships amongst sangomas in not something new but began a long time ago when female sangomas used to have 'ancestral wives'." In other words, scholars like Mnyadi (2020) and Nkabinde and Morgan (2011) link homosexuality to African indigenous knowledge systems. Therefore, GALA was purposively selected in this study to understand how it is using orality in the form of oral history and oral traditions in documenting those stories that speak to homosexuality as not alien to Africa. One can say, in that way, GALA is using Africanisation as an epistemological tool in understanding homosexuality. GALA is also decolonising its archive, which used to be more white than black during the apartheid era. This again is done through the promotion, documentation, and preservation of black queer oral archive. GALA has also managed to interchangeably use Africanisation, decolonisation, and Eurocentric archival practices in telling the South African queer story.

Contextualising the emergence of the Gay and Lesbian Memory in Action

GALA is a South African community archive with tentacles throughout the Southern African region, primarily serving the LGBTI communities. It is a dynamic archive that has taken various roles, such as an archive, community centre, art therapy facilitator, and publisher (Sizemore-Barber, 2017). It provides a theoretical opportunity to understand queer community archives in the global South vis-à-vis the Global North. The existence of GALA in Africa is proof of resilience because queer community archives are a rare spectacle considering the prevalent public homophobic tendencies, including sometimes officially sanctioned anti-LGBTI restrictive legislation. Sizemore-Barber (2017) notes that GALA is the "only" LGBTI archive in Africa. It is not only into the preservation of historical records but is also prioritising contemporary projects, many of which are motivated by the need for social justice interventions in some of the most marginalised constituencies of the LGBTI community. It also places a strong focus on the production and dissemination of content in the form of publications and booklets, research reports, books, conference papers, exhibitions, and training materials to support the LGBTI communities. It has successfully deployed oral history epistemology in addressing contemporary challenges faced by the LGBTI communities in South Africa. It also exemplifies how a colonial and postcolonial archive that ignored their stories can be countered by the establishment of a parallel epistemic centre in the form of a GALA community archive.

The formation of the LGBTI community archives has sometimes been driven by the fact that mainstream archives since the colonial era have struggled to document and tell their stories. This is a fact recognised by Koskovich (2016, p. 2) when he argues that "LGBTI people similarly saw scant reflection of their own past in museums, public monuments, local historical societies, and the popular history distributed by mainstream media, let alone at officially recognised historic places." The scantiness of the LGBTI archive during the apartheid era can be attributed to the nationalist ideological climate of the dispensation, which was conservative Calvinist and Christian, while, at the same time, against the queer community through a combination of Afrikaner Calvinism and Christian Nationalist ideology (Muller, 2019, p. 5). This ideology promoted hegemonic Afrikaner masculinity, morality, sexual purity, and heteronormativity (Retief, 1994). Muller (2019, p. 10), citing Du Pisani (2001), argues that "the perceived femininity and/or inferiority of queer subjects, therefore, marks them as 'un-Afrikaans' and existing 'outside tradition and culture and thus outside the nation'." The Muller (2019) article shows how the apartheid police photographed LGBTI individuals and used that photograph archive to humiliate them in the public media. As a result, they were forced to become invisible because visibility and violence highlight the lives of LGBTI people. Such an environment obviously led to the apartheid state archives ignoring the stories of the LGBTI. The formation of GALA can then be attributed to the scantiness of its history in the public domain. However, it should be realised that the politically anti-LGBTI unfriendly environment did not totally suppress their archive, as noted by Peach (2005, p. 107) who explains "that white, black, and coloured South African Queer histories have always existed in sections of the broader community, but were often hidden not just from the mainstream, but also from each other."

Sustainability of community archives benchmarking GALA as a model

Community archives need to be sustainable so that they can really be considered as an alternative epistemic space that can be used by indigenous communities to archive their stories. One of the major impediments to achieving sustainability is the lack of an identifiable and consistent organisational structure. Proper governance issues are usually associated with a clear organisational structure. Dysfunction quickly steps in when issues of organisational structure are ignored. The importance of a proper organisational structure can be gleaned from Nene and Pillay (2019, p. 10), who state that

> in any organisation, one of the most valuable assets is considered to be the person within that organization. For the effectiveness and alignment of personnel with the organisation's vision, it is of utmost importance to have leadership and management systems and personnel that are effective and efficient in ensuring... sustainability.

It is very unfortunate that some of the emerging community archives on the African continent lack this attribute. Most of them become one-man organisations, as was observed in this research. Such community archives exist only because of the passion and commitment of one or two individuals. A few lessons can be learnt from GALA's organisational structure that has made its sustainability possible. It has a consistent and identifiable organisational structure that consists of the Director, Administration Officer, Archives Coordinator, Programmes Coordinator, Senior Information Officer, GALA Intern, and Youth Forum Coordinator (GALA, 2022). It also has a board of trustees who govern and decide on all essential matters relating to the administration, finances, and strategic direction of the organisation. These are listed as follows in GALA (2022): Melanie Judge, Mwenya Kabwe, Zethu Matebeni (Chairperson), Getti Mercorio, Thabo Msibi, and Kendall Petersen. It also has patrons such as Justice Edwin Cameron and the late Archbishop Emeritus Desmond Tutu. Therefore, this study clearly revealed that GALA has an established organisational structure. It is not a one-man show. It does not only have a board of trustees, but also renowned patrons such as Justice Edwin Cameron (a legal judge well known for HIV/AIDS and gay rights activism), and it once had the late Archbishop Emeritus Desmond Tutu (who was awarded a Nobel Prize for Peace in 1984 for his role in the opposition to apartheid in South Africa).

When one talks of organisational structures, what comes to mind for the colonised are Eurocentric management systems such as the Weberian model. However, some Africans forget that, for centuries, African societies have enjoyed a tradition of participatory democracy in their organisational structures (Mbigi, 2007). Mbigi (2007, p. 299) continues to argue that "the organisational structure of indigenous African systems was generally based on kingship and ancestry...." Each ethnic group had its own system of government. These were unwritten constitutions like the Constitution of Britain. "Customs and traditions established the governance procedures." The hallmark of the African management system lies in its emphasis on consensus and freedom of speech in which minority voices are even heard and listened to (Mbigi, 2007, p. 300), as was the case with "edale" (the Nguni word for the traditional African courts mostly found in Southern Africa). Moyo and Ncube (2010, p. 41) echo the same sentiments by stating that

> in the pre-colonial Ndebele society, political decisions were discussed in *"edale"* and *"ebandla"*, the highest council of state, and without this cherished institution, a king could not make any decision of national importance. Many representatives would gather for consultative discussions in the determination of national policy if national policy representatives were a worldly-wise group. *"Idale"* as a public forum recognised that leadership could not make unilateral decisions and that leaders could only exist within a collective milieu. Since the fundamental matters concerning the welfare of the nation are studied, deliberated, and made collectively after consensus.

As a result, the community archives, being an organisation led by one man, is diametrically opposed to Africa's collective and consensus organisational structures. Perhaps this is one of the reasons why African community archives fail to be sustainable. It should be noted, however, that the authors of this book are not advocating for the golden utopian past and rejecting the present or Western ways of knowing, but rather for the by-product of all ways of knowing that are hospitable to African epistemologies. In that vein, the argument is that community archives attempting to preserve the story of indigenous Africans can do so more effectively by drawing on both Western management philosophies and African traditional ones. Much can be learned from how GALA has structured its organisation while drawing on African management philosophies. In other words, community archives must be managed by consensus from the community, while also embracing the African philosophy of Ubuntu/humanism and having a core, clear, and identifiable person running the community archive on a daily basis.

GALA's archival holdings

Since they are aimed at the subaltern, community archives in the global South, particularly in Southern Africa, are dominated by oral records and artefacts. According to Bhebhe (2019, p. 13), "generally speaking, minority groups can be classified as subaltern, and it is assumed that in most cases such kinds of group of people have no archives to talk about." Ndlovu-Gatsheni (2007, p. 11) contends that "since the subaltern has no archives, all their concerns can only be well captured through oral testimonies and tradition." However, this should not be taken as always being the case, because there are a number of community archives in Southern Africa, such as the GALA, that have a massive written archive. According to a study conducted by Bhebhe (2019), GALA "has over 180 collections, ranging in size from one file to over 150 archive boxes." These collections are made up primarily of organisational material from LGBTI organisations and campaigns (about 50% of the material) and personal collections (about 30% of the material), which include letters, diaries, photographs, and memorabilia. The research discovered that some of the written archives are from cultural events and marches, covering events and organisations such as the Out in Africa Film Festival, various pride marches, theatre performances, exhibitions, and literature, and these are split across various collections in addition to a press collection dating back to the 1980s (Bhebhe, 2019). Another collection, 'Archiving Gala' includes various GALA projects, as well as their own individual collections. Interestingly, a 2019 interviewee revealed that some of these archival accumulations begin as oral history programmes and then lead to exhibitions and book publications, which then feed back into the archive, accounting for up to 20% of archive material. This further emphasises the importance of oral history in community archiving. Bhebhe (2019) discovered in the same study that GALA also accumulates its archive through donations from both individuals and organisations (mostly those that have ceased to function). According to the participant who was interviewed:

> Significant individual collections include those of activists such as Simon Nkoli, Edwin Cameron, Beverly Ditsie, and Zackie Achmat. Their organisational records include those of the National Coalition for Gay & Lesbian Equality (NCGLE), GALA's largest collections, as well as South Africa's first black gay and lesbian organization, the Gay and Lesbian Organisation of the Witwatersrand (GLOW), and that of the Gays & Lesbians of Zimbabwe (GALZ), which is housed with GALA for safekeeping due to the homophobic political climate in Zimbabwe. The organisational records include meeting minutes, campaign documents, newsletters, promotional material, posters, and T-shirts.

The mix of records, including oral history and artefacts, is not uncommon in community archiving, particularly in a queer archive, as Danbolt (2009, p. 35) observes that an ideal queer archive should be an "eclectic merging of ethnographic oral history, online database and home pages, collections of zines and temporary artefacts."

According to Bhebhe (2019), the motivation for using oral history, as mentioned by the research participant, is that

> until the mid-1990s, LGBTI activism in South Africa was largely dominated by white activists and organisations, and the natural consequence of this is that these people and organisations have a larger presence in the GALA archive. We are an archive in South Africa and therefore, the politics of race is heavily present and cannot be ignored. GALA has actively sought to try to flesh out our white-dominated history with the roles and stories of black activists as well as the everyday lives and experiences of queer black South Africans. Due to the lack of formal organisations as a consequence of the realities of apartheid, there is little in terms of tangible archival history, unlike for white organisations like the Gay Association of South Africa (GASA). GALA has, therefore, undertaken various oral history projects to try to record these stories before they are lost.

It may appear that "the GALA's motivation for using oral history in documenting the queer stories is that until the late 1990s, LGBTI activists were mainly from the white population. The stories of black activists were silenced" (Bhebhe 2019). Therefore, this massive archival collection at GALA can be attributed to the fact that this community archive has an organisational post dedicated to an archivist who mainly does archiving. The other reason is the fact that some of the programmes run by the GALA in turn contribute to the archive during their lifespan.

Community's archival oral history programmes in addressing contemporary issues

Archival Platform (2018, p. 60) contends that GALA's oral history projects are an important point of convergence for archival collecting, project-based research, dissemination, and knowledge construction. Oral histories create archival collections, serve as the nucleus of many of GALA's research initiatives, and provide content for dissemination activities such as publications and exhibitions. The collection policy of oral history reflects an organisational position on struggles for historical justice as well as more pressing contemporary social and political issues. These interests and objectives are frequently inextricably linked, as evidenced by past and ongoing oral history projects (Archival Platform, 2018, p. 60).

The majority of South African community archives' oral history programmes focus on marginalised and neglected histories. GALA's website, for example, mentions having "commissioned an oral history project which will capture the narratives of Queer and LGBTIQ students, many of whom felt increasingly excluded during the 2015/16 #FeesMustFall protests as a result of hetero patriarchy...." This research is concerned with documenting the protestors' experiences while demonstrating their presence and impact during the protests. It also describes the participants' involvement and the outcomes of their involvement in order to ensure that their stories are not lost (GALA, 2020). Another programme addressing current issues is the Deaf LGBTI oral history project (Meletse & Morgan, 2012). According to Sizemore-Barber (2017, p. 128), the programme began as an outreach project for deaf MSM (Men who have Sex with Men), then expanded to use a variety of tactics – theatre, comic books, peer education, online life stories – to educate deaf students and schools about HIV. According to Nell and Shapiro (2011, p. 38), GALA has "played a special role in addressing the needs of LGBTI people with disabilities because it has a deaf staff member who has drawn attention to what it means to be further marginalised among the marginalised."

Another programme mentioned on the GALA (2016) website is that of documenting the stories of GALA youth, which the institution felt were underrepresented in the region. Other oral history projects in which GALA is involved include the Holy Trinity Church, which involves a group of LGBTIQ migrants who meet at the Holy Trinity Catholic Church in Braamfontein – their stories as queer migrants in Johannesburg, and their relationship with the Church are then documented. According to GALA (2020):

> Established in 2009, the LGBTIQ ministry provides a safe and inclusive space for LGBTIQ migrants, refugees, and asylum seekers in need of spiritual and/or psychosocial support. Holy Trinity's commitment to providing pastoral care to people on the margins – particularly those facing violence because of their sexuality, gender, ethnicity and/or documentation status – marks it out as a unique site in South Africa's religious landscape.

The sanctuary's oral history programme seeks to celebrate Holy Trinity's contribution to human rights by preserving the memories and reflections of those involved with the LGBTIQ ministry (GALA, 2020). The project seeks to document the lived experiences of LGBTIQ migrants, refugees, and asylum seekers and to better understand how these individuals navigate state structures, develop livelihood strategies, and form solidarity networks (GALA, 2020). The church also pays a nominal rent for them to use the GALA library as a meeting place, a place safe from xenophobic and homophobic climates where they can share their stories (Nell & Shapiro, 2011, p. 38).

It should be noted that some of these oral history programmes are addressing contemporary challenges. Their oral history discourse is not based on pre-independence stories alone but is also contemporary. This is reinforced by the participant's statement that GALA is also attempting to better "capture 'history in the making', with a focus on what we call the 'Contemporary Archive', thereby not waiting for individuals and/or organisations to donate material, but to capture events as they happen, as far as capacity and funds allow."

GALA's emphasis on using oral history in current issues runs counter to the general discourse of oral history in South Africa, which tends to be "history from above, created and told from the perspectives and experiences of a small and powerful minority" (McKinley & Veriava, 2008, p. 2). It is a history that "predominately emanates out of the institutional frameworks and processes within which elites operate, constantly being told through the voices and agencies of those who possess political, economic, social, and cultural power and position" (McKinley & Veriava, 2008, p. 2). "Effectively then, it is a 'history' of, by, and through an elite that relates mainly to state and corporate institutions, elitist societal processes, and macro-nationalist narratives" (McKinley & Veriava, 2008, p. 2). Its bias is constantly refracted through the lens of the pre-1994 past (that is, the 'liberation struggle,' the negotiations process, and/or leading figures and movements in them) (McKinley & Veriava, 2008, p. 2).

It is against this background that GALA is telling the story of LGBTI communities in South Africa after being neglected by government institutions. On top of that, unlike mainstream archival institutions in South Africa that are elitist in their approach, telling the liberation history of those cadres who are now in power after defeating the apartheid system, the GALA has gone a step further and used oral history as a tool to address contemporary challenges. That mentality, which presumes South African history to be something that relates predominately to the pre-Independence 1994 era, has been ignored in community archives such as GALA, as they target social contemporary challenges that are faced by LGBTI communities. So, the idea that, analytically, "the post-apartheid 1994 period, since it remains fluid and contemporary (in the classical historical sense), is thus seen as having no end and therefore no basis for enjoying historical status" (McKinley & Veriava, 2008, p. 3) is critically challenged by GALA, as seen by such programmes like #Fees Must Fall.

It can then be deduced that community archives are able to embark on specific programmes that are tailored to address specific problems. Their constituencies are manageable in terms of size, and they have the advantage of sharing the same interests. This is unlike the mainstream national archives or museums, which have large, diverse constituencies that have diverse interests and the burden of being politically correct. Access to the GALA's archive, including its oral history holdings, became very pronounced when it reinvented itself from the Gay and Lesbian Archive to the Gay and Lesbian Memory in Action. Access to archival holdings is one of the cornerstones of proper archival management. Winn (2015, p. 7) argues that access is a product of both physical and intellectual availability, reflecting the ability of researchers to find and explore records both in person and online. This is usually achieved by the existence of finding aids and inventories, and there should be no excessive restrictions, as this would defeat the purpose of access. It is against this background that the community, including mainstream archives, strives to provide access to their holdings.

Oral history records are primarily accessed by academics and other researchers in mainstream archival institutions, but not by minority groups or local community members from whom some collections originate (Bhebhe, 2019). In South Africa, the question of access is very important, as it is still battling the colonial legacies in which old institutions denied access to the marginalised communities. In the case of the queer archive, issues pertaining to access become more important because LGBTI communities rarely appear in the national official archive unless "as statistics collected to appeal to funders" to the extent that the African Queer has disappeared into a mass of acronyms. Therefore, Sizemore-Barber (2017, p. 118) calls for archival strategies that multiply marginalised individuals.

However, it should be noted that GALA is not only providing access to the archival collections but also a safe meeting place for the LGBTI community. It is more than an archive, as it is also a library and a community centre, where it becomes a place to meet. Nell and Shapiro (2011, p. 37) describe this scenario in the following terms:

> Situated at the University of the Witwatersrand, GALA is housed in an unassuming set of offices at University Corner in Braamfontein, Johannesburg. The library is a crowded, book-lined space with a table and chairs inviting discussion. It provides a place where people can meet and discuss – and it has

nurtured groups and fora that have themselves since become fully-fledged organisations.

Archival Platform (2018, p. 64) argues that the impact of GALA's work has seen an increase in the diversity of GALA's user base and an increase in the number of South Africans using the archival collections on projects relating to sexual orientation and gender identity; a large body of academic research to which the archival collections have contributed, as seen in analysing the sources of what has been published on LGBTI issues; and focused contributions to research, education, and training that support and position GALA's work in relation to an ongoing LGBTI and human rights social movement. The online repositories are slowly establishing a footprint in the archival space of South Africa. Some of the examples are the Bafokeng Digital Archive and the Ulwazi Programme. GALA is yet to fully embrace such an approach.

Conclusion

To conclude, the GALA has left its mark on the African continent as one of the most vibrant and functional LGBTI archives. All of this is taking place on a continent that is still struggling to embrace LGBTI people at a social and cultural level. GALA's archive is very eclectic as it houses different kinds of archives, including oral history testimonies. It does not only see history as pre-independence but also as contemporary. As this chapter demonstrated, such an approach has enabled GALA to use oral history epistemology to address contemporary challenges confronting LGBTI communities. GALA also managed to decolonise South Africa's LGBTI archive without interfering with the National Archives and Records Services of South Africa. This can serve as a model for the African continent in terms of how community archives can be used to decolonise and indigenise black people's stories.

References

Archival Platform. (2018). A ground of struggle: four decades of archival activism in South Africa. Available at: http://archivalplatform.org (Accessed 16 May 2022).

Bhebhe, S. (2015). Description of the oral history programme at the National Archives of Zimbabwe. *Oral History Australia Journal*, 37: 49–55. Available at: https://oralhistoryaustralia.org.au/wp-content/uploads/2015_journal_full.pdf (Accessed 12 April 2022).

Bhebhe, S. (2016). Interrogating Thompson's community approach to oral history with special reference to selected oral history programmes in Zimbabwe. *Oral History Journal of South Africa*, 4(2): 1–15. https://doi.org/10.25159/2309-5792/687

Bhebhe, S. (2017). Makhokhoba and the surrounding areas as the remarkable centres of liberation struggle in Zimbabwe: a case of *Zhii* protests. *Oral history Journal of South Africa*, 5(1): 1–22. https://doi.org/10.25159/2309-5792/1876

Bhebhe, S. (2019). *Memorialising minority groups in post-independence Zimbabwe and South Africa: a critical analysis of oral history programme*. PhD thesis, Pretoria: University of South Africa.

Bhebhe, S. and Khumalo, N.B. (2019). Trends in the utilization of the holdings at the Bulawayo Archives and Records Centre, Zimbabwe (2014-2017). In P. Ngulube (Ed.), *Handbook of research on advocacy, promotion, and public programming for memory institutions*. Hershey: IGL Global, pp. 144–159. doi:10.4018/978-1-5225-7429-3.ch008

Bhebhe, S., and Ngoepe, M. (2022). Political and socio-economic dynamics on the access to oral sources at national archives in Zimbabwe and South Africa. *Collections*, 18(2): 176–201. https://doi.org/10.1177/15501906211052716

Chirikure, S., Manyanga, M., Ndoro, W. and Pwiti, G. (2010). Unfulfilled promises? Heritage management and community participation at some of Africa's cultural heritage sites. *International Journal of Heritage Studies*, 16(2): 30–44. doi:10.1080/13527250903441739

Chitando, E. and Mateveke, P. (2017). Africanizing the discourse on homosexuality: challenges and prospects, *Critical African Studies*, 9(1): 124–140. doi:10.1080/21681392.2017.1285243

Choudry, A. and Vally, S. (2018). Learning from, in, and with independent community and activist archives: the past in our present and future. *Education as Change*, 32 (2): 1–9. https://doi.org/10.25159/1947-9417/4513

Danbolt, M. (2009). *Touching history: archival relations in queer art and theory*. Nikolaj: Copenhagen Contemporary Art Centre.

Du Pisani, K. (2001). Puritanism transformed: Afrikaner masculinities in the apartheid and post-apartheid period. In R. Morrell (Ed.), *Changing men in Southern Africa*, Pietermaritzburg: University of Natal Press and London: Zed Books.

Epprecht, M. (2004). *Hungochani: The history of a dissident sexuality in Southern Africa*. Montreal: McGill-Queen's University Press.

Flinn, A. and Stevens, M. (2009). "It is noh mistri, wi mekin histri": telling our own story: Independent and community archives in the UK, challenging and subverting the mainstream. In J. Bastian and B. Alexander (Eds.), *Community archives: the shaping of memory*, London: Facet Publishing, pp. 3–27.

Gibbons, L. (2019). Connecting personal and community memory-making: Facebook groups as emergent community archives. In *Proceedings of RAILS –Research Applications Information and Library Studies, 2018, Faculty of Information Technology, Monash University, 28-30 November 2018. Information Research*, 24(3). Available at: http://InformationR.net/ir/24-3/rails/rails1804.html (Accessed 2 April 2022).

Harrison, A. (2021). "I can't wait for you to die": a community archives critique. *Archivaria*, 92(Fall): 110–137.

Ibrahim, A.M. (2015). LGBT rights in Africa and the discursive role of international human rights law. *African Human Rights Law Journal* 15: 263–281. http://dx.doi.org/10.17159/1996-2096/2015/v15n2a2]

Katsetse, E.D. and Namono, C. (2019). It's not gelling: conservation mitigation at Bonne Esperance 016 Rock Art Site, Makgabeng, South Africa. *Conservation and Management of Archaeological Sites*, 21(5-6): 344–365, doi:10.1080/13505033.2021.1893480

Kaunda, C.J. (2013). *A threat to Zulu patriarchy and the continuation of community: a queer analysis of same sex relationships amongst Female Traditional Healers at Inanda and KwaNgcolosi, KwaZulu-Natal.* Dissertation at the University of KwaZulu Natal, Durban.

Koskovich, G. (2016). The history of queer history: one hundred years of the search for shared heritage. In M.E. Springate (Ed.), *LGBTQ America: A theme study of lesbian, gay, bisexual, transgender, and queer history*, Washington D.C: National Park Foundation, pp. 1–44.

Madsen, W. (2015). Using the past to strengthen the present: intersections between oral history and community resilience. *Oral History Australia Journal*, 37: 56–62.

Mbigi, L. (2007). Spirit of African leadership: a comparative African perspective. In K. April and M. Shockley (Eds.), *Diversity new realities in a changing world*. Hampshire: Palgrave Macmillan, pp. 294–304. Available at: https://link.springer.com/content/pdf/10.1057/9780230627 529.pdf (Accessed 10 May 2022).

McKinley, D.T. and Veriava, A. (2008). *Forgotten' voices in the present: alternative, post-1994 oral histories from three poor communities in South Africa*. Braamfontein: S.P. Design.

Meletse, J. and Morgan, R. (2012). "I believe in myself and I am a strong deaf gay (person)": an oral history project with deaf gay and lesbian South Africans. Available at: https://gala.co.za/wpcontent/uploads/2018/01/Deaf_gay_life_stories_MeletseMorgan_WFD_2011.pdf (Accessed 20 May 2022).

Moran, J. (2016). To spread the revolution: anarchist archives and libraries. In M. Morrone (Ed.), *Informed agitation: library and information skills in social justice movements and beyond.* Sacramento: Library Juice Press, pp. 173–184. Available at: https://libcom.org/article/spread-revolution-anarchist-archives-and-libraries-jessica-moran (Accessed 13 April 2022).

Moyo, T. and Ncube, B. (2010). An analysis of the relevance of Ndebele political wisdom as reflected in their proverbs. *Journal of Language & Communication*, 4(1): 36–49. Available at: https://eds.p.ebscohost.com/eds/pdfviewer/pdfviewer?vid=1&sid=b6988853-3f0b-47bb-96a6-c4db71aa869e%40redis (Accessed 12 May 2022).

Mnyadi, K. (2020). The influence of ancestral spirits on sexual identity amongst Traditional Healers (iZangoma) in South Africa: A discourse analysis, *Inkanyiso, Journal Human & Social Science* 12 (2): 159–177.

Muller, B.M. (2019). Under Priscilla's eyes: state violence against South Africa's queer community during and after apartheid. *Image & Text*, 33: 1–36. doi:http://dx.doi.org/10.17159/2617-3255/2018/n33a11

Namono, C. (2018). Digital technology and a community framework for heritage rock art tourism, Makgabeng Plateau, South Africa. *African Archaeological Review*, 35: 269–284. https://doi.org/10.1007/s10437-018-9298-y

Ndlovu-Gatsheni, J. (2007). *In search of common ground: oral history, human rights and the United Nations (UN) Human Rights Council.* Paper presented at the international conference on human Rights and Social Justice: Setting the Agenda for the United Nations Human Rights Council: An international forum on: War affected children, Gender Rights and Rights of indigenous peoples. University of Winnipeg, Canada, 23–25 February.

Nell, M. and Shapiro, J. (2011). Out of the box: queer youth in South Africa today. Available at: www.atlanticphilanthropies.org/wpcontent/uploads/2015/09/Out_of_the_box_queer_youth_in_South_Africa_Today_0.pdf (Accessed 4 May 2022).

Nene, S.W. and Pillay, A.S. (2019). An investigation of the impact of organisational structure on organisational performance. *Financial Risk and Management Reviews*, 5(1): 10–24. https://doi.org/10.18488/journal.89.2019.51.10.24

Netshakhuma, N.S. (2020). The role of archives in documenting African National Congress Women's League records that impacted the development of their records 1960-1990. *Global Knowledge, Memory and Communication*, 70(1/2): 44–59. doi:10.1108/GKMC-09-2019-0107

Ngoepe, M. and Setumu, T. (2016). Converting oral narratives into written literature: lessons learnt from heritage projects undertaken in the Makgabeng area, Limpopo, South Africa. *Mousaion*, 34(4): 15–29.

Nkabinde, N. and Morgan, R. (2011). This has happened since ancient times ... it's something that you are born with': ancestral wives among same-sex sangomas in South Africa. *Agenda*, 20(67): 9–19. doi:10.1080/10130950.2006.9674693

Peach, R. (2005). *Queer cinema as a fifth cinema in South Africa and Australia*. PhD thesis, Sydney: University of Technology. Available at: https://opus.lib.uts.edu.au/bitstream/10453/20344/5/02whole.pdf (Accessed 15 May 2022).

Pikela, H., Thondhlana, T.P. and Madlome, S.K. (2022) Towards community-driven curatorship: traditional chiefs and cultural connoisseurs at the Avuxeni community museum, Chiredzi south district. In T.T.P. Hondhlana, J. Mataga and D. Munjeri (Eds.), *Independent museums and culture centres in colonial and post-colonial Zimbabwe: non-state players, local communities, and self-representation*, London: Routledge. doi:10.4324/9781003108238-16

Retief, G. (1994). Keeping Sodom out of the laager: state repression of homosexuality in apartheid South Africa. In M. Gevisser and E. Cameron (Eds.), *Defiant desire: gay and lesbian lives in South Africa*, New York: Routledge, p. 99–114.

Saleh, R. (2017). *Archives, archiving and the marginalised: a reflection of South Africa*. Paper presented at Arxius per la Democràcia i Dret a la Informació VIII Jornades de l'Associació d'Arxivers i Gestors de Documents Valencians València, 26–27 d'octubre de.

Scott, B. (2014). Lowveld practices in Mahenye, Zimbabwe: a critical analysis of resilience in a marginalized Southern African Community. Available at: https://scholarworks.umt.edu/etd/4381 (Accessed 10 May 2022).

Setumu, T. (2010). *Communal identity creation among the Makgabeng rural people in Limpopo Province*. PhD Thesis, Turfloop: University of Limpopo.

Sheffield, R. (2017). Community archives. *Currents of archival thinking*, ABC-Clio, Santa Barbara and Denver, pp. 351–376.

Sizemore-Barber, A. (2017). Archival movements – South Africa's Gay and Lesbian Memory in Action. *The Journal of South Africa and American Studies*, 18(2): 117–130. http://dx.doi.org/10.1080/17533171.2016.1270568

Suttner, R. (2007). Women in the ANC-led underground. In N. Gasa (Ed.), *Basus 'imbokodo Wawel 'imilambo: Women Making History in South Africa*, Cape Town: HSRC, 233–256.

Tribbett, K., Vo Dang, T., Yun, A.E. and Zavala, J. (2020). *Transforming knowledge transforming libraries – researching the intersections of ethnic studies and community archives: Final report.* Available at: https://escholarship.org/uc/item/47c2h0dd

Winn, S.R. (2015). Ethics of access in displaced archives. *Provenance Journal of the Society of Georgia Archivists* 33(1): 6–13. Available at: http://digitalcommons.kennesaw.edu/provenance/vol33/iss1/5 (Accessed 15 May 2022).

6 Sustainable structures for indigenous archives in the postcolonial context

Introduction

This chapter expands on the previous chapters' argument about the need for sustainable structures for community archives dedicated to bringing black people's stories to light. It is important to establish how indigenous archives can be created and sustained for the restoration and preservation of hidden memories, as well as to ensure continuity in their management. The assumption that influences the shape of the sustainable archival structure is that the indigenous peoples' mistrust of state and institutional archives, demands for control of archives, as well as the establishment of autonomous archival spaces, are all thought to contribute to the important and fraught process of decolonising settler colonial archives (Luker, 2017). In other words, this chapter takes note of those archives that are outside the mainstream archival setup and tries to endeavour how they can be integrated into a sustainable organisational structure. It should be noted that it is not always the case that community archives should be integrated into the national archival system, but where it happens, they should not be subjugated or swallowed but maintain at least a semblance of independence. Therefore, this chapter presents different scenarios in which a structure that respects the independence of community archives can be visualised.

Naturally fluid indigenous archival structures

Naturally fluid indigenous archival structures are those that still maintain the traditional setup of how our African societies have

DOI: 10.4324/9781003277989-7

preserved their knowledge since time immemorial. The call for the preservation of indigenous knowledge stems from the fact that Africa has been able to generate, test, and apply indigenous knowledge through its own methodologies and approaches. This knowledge has sustained communities for years prior to colonialism, which somehow downplayed the value of indigenous knowledge and promoted Western knowledge systems (Khumalo & Baloyi, 2017, p. 1). Colonialism engendered reliance on Western knowledge systems, and Africa has long ignored its own rich indigenous knowledge (Khumalo & Baloyi, 2017, p. 1). Therefore, there are now these spirited efforts from different stakeholders to preserve this knowledge. The indigenous archives can be preserved orally in people's heads, as has been the case for a long time. Some of the traditional living custodians of this indigenous knowledge prefer that it should be preserved in its natural form, as Maluleka (2017, p. 172) found out and reported that the

> findings also suggest that some healers believe that it is the responsibility of the ancestors to preserve knowledge of traditional healing. They believe that the ancestors keep the knowledge safe until they identify someone deserving so that they can pass it on to them. This crop of healers is against the documentation of this knowledge. They indicated that they knew everything by heart because it was shown to them in their dreams, and they still have that picture of their dream in their heads. They mostly identify their herbs through smell, taste, weight, and colour.

Unfortunately, this naturally fluid orality and word-of-mouth preservation is facing challenges from modernity. This natural kind of preservation needs to be reactivated and promoted among black people. Reactivation can be done by the government in introducing oral traditions into the curricula of students at all levels as part of the decolonisation process. This rejuvenation in the use of indigenous knowledge is motivated by the fact that the

> elders are very concerned about the loss of traditional knowledge due to their inability to transmit it to future generations owing to, inter alia, loss of language, oral nature of the

knowledge, and young people's perception of traditional knowledge as obsolete.

(Maina, 2012, p. 16)

Writing about the importance of the preservation of the traditionally powerful and sacred chant called *Kapata*, Rahmam and Letlora (2018) suggest that the government of Indonesia needs to include it in the educational curriculum for it to be preserved. This idea is supported by Ngoepe (2022, p. 5), who argues that

> we should rather, through the government, focus on a 30-year experimental programme where indigenous schools are established with a full IKS programme from astrology to medicine, with the learners starting at Grade R, sponsored by the government over a period of time from primary school to secondary school to tertiary level until placement in the workplace.

Instead of collecting these oral traditions, which are repositories of African wisdom, and archiving them in public archives, the impetus should be on inculcating those cultural virtues into the people's heads. Our traditional custodians such as *oMakhulu* and *rakgadi/makadzi* (these are grandmothers and aunts who, from our African ontological foundations, used to transfer the wisdom and knowledge of the past to the present generation) need to be incorporated into the contemporary education systems in Africa (Magoqwana, 2021). This will lead to the creation of fluid archives that are not fixed in archival institutions but rather the mobility of those indigenous archives within people's heads and thereby their preservation. This agrees with Masuku and Pasipamire's argument (2014, p. 122) that

> IK is preserved through practice. In other words, IK taken away from its people, community, or practitioners is no longer IK. Thus, IK is an ethnographical issue that is preserved through practice. Therefore, any effort by librarians and archivists in trying to document and preserve IK is a sheer waste of time and resources. The question is: why try to document something that is not documentable? Is this not a waste of time and effort? Although others may argue that IK is likely to be extinct if not documented, for example, as the bearers of this knowledge die,

we believe that, because IK is non-static in nature, that which is necessary for the community or people to know and is relevant to their lives at that particular time, will always stand the test of time.

This argument by Masuku and Pasipamire (2014) sits well with the view that the African archival epistemologies will be awkwardly accommodated in the Eurocentric archival structures as they are strange and 'incompatible' bedfellows. Battiste and Henderson (2000) make it clear that traditional indigenous knowledge is a distinct knowledge system that does not match the existing academic categories of Eurocentric knowledge. Even though Te Awhina Ka'al – Mahuta (2012) writes about the indigenous archives of the Māori, the first people accept that the creation of their online digital archives is not a replacement of their oral traditions, as these continue to live with them on a daily basis. Te Awhina Ka'al – Mahuta (2012) succinctly puts this argument by arguing that

> memory is still the most important vessel for the survival of Māori culture and tradition. The digital repository is not intended to replace memory or the oral tradition. It is hoped that the digital repository will sit alongside oral tradition in a complementary way and act as a resource to supplement the continued oral traditions of Māori.

Marschall (2014) expresses similar sentiments, arguing that, despite the positive benefits that communities gain from participating in online digital heritage projects, the issue is that this can be viewed as more of a heritagisation of lived local culture. This can lead to a process whereby the communities, instead of viewing their culture as being continuous and lived, may just end up thinking that their ways of living are heritage that needs to be preserved. Marschall (2014) further argues that safeguarding of their culture can therefore have a potentially negative influence on Intangible Cultural Heritage (ICH) communities by altering local views about change and innovation in living traditions and how they relate to the past.

Some scholars, such as Onyima (2016, p. 289), call for the hosting of state cultural festivals that will promote the oral African archive, and this will lead to the inculcation of cultural heritage into younger generations. In Zimbabwe, cultural festivals such as *Intwasa* should be encouraged and promoted. *Intwasa* is a multi-disciplinary arts festival that brings together various art forms such as dance, theatre, music, film, literary arts, visual arts, spoken word, and fashion within one platform (Intwasa ARTS Festival KoBulawayo, 2022). Such national festivals can create a moving archive within the population. The Blouberg-Makgabeng-Senwabarwana (BMS) arts and culture festival is one such festival happening at a local level. People in this area sing and dance at weddings, thanksgiving ceremonies for their ancestors, and regular get-togethers to drink beer (Ngoepe & Setumu, 2016).

According to Setumu (2016), the BMS Arts and Culture Festivals was a 12-month project (June 2015–May 2016) funded by the national DAC and implemented by MAK HERP, a heritage publishing company (the reader is referred to Figure 3.1 for an example of cultural festival activities where oral history in its natural setting is performed). In line with the Department of Arts and Culture's Mzansi Golden Economy, which aims to enhance economic development and social cohesion through using cultural and creative industries, the main aim of the project was to strengthen the arts, culture, and heritage sectors by identifying, developing, promoting, and documenting indigenous dance, music, and storytelling within the Blouberg local municipal area.

The heritage and culture of the BMS area vary. In some instances, communities were engaged in such initiatives (Ngoepe & Setumu, 2016; Setumu, 2015), including the Makgabeng Career Expo and Heritage Celebration; Blouberg, Makgabeng, and Senwabarwana Cultural Festivals; Malebogo-Boer War documentary and historical drama; Dikgaatwanetša Makgabeng (rock art paintings); and Makgabeng-Setlaole Heritage (folktales, clan praises, conducting funerals, and beliefs). Products of some of these projects include CDs of traditional music, folktales, and riddles that are played on a local radio station, Blouberg FM streaming at 95.0 MHz, which mostly focuses on heritage and cultural content, including oral history.

The preservation of indigenous archives calls for all hands on the deck. The governments of Africa, with the support of such continental institutions as the African Union, need to encourage their populations to value themselves in terms of their African identity. This is likely to be a challenge because the effects of colonisation were far more than merely physical, as they also had and continue to have a corrosive effect on the mind of a black person. The effects of colonialism are still with us today because of its "perverted logic." It turns its attention to the past of the colonised people and distorts it, disfigures it, and destroys it (Fanon, 2001, p. 211) so that we (the black people) begin to hate our identity and start yearning to be white in our mannerisms. The mental effects are seen in small issues such as naming, whereby after years of the physical conclusion of colonisation, one finds that black parents continue giving their children English names. Even worse, the *nouveau riche* has even abandoned their indigenous languages in home setup to the extent that they now communicate with their children in English or other colonial languages. This desire by black people to become white will always be a barrier that must be overcome if we are to reclaim our oral tradition. Falola (2017) refers to the African archive as "our ritual archive." Falola (2017, p. 703), cited by Magoqwana (2021, p. 93), defines this ritual archive as

> words as well as texts, ideas, symbols, shrines, images, performances, and indeed objects that document as well as speak to those religious experiences and practices that allow us to understand the African world through various bodies of philosophies, literatures, languages, histories and much more. By implication, ritual archives are huge, unbounded in scale and scope, storing tremendous amounts of data on both natural and supernatural agents, ancestors, gods, good and bad witches, life, death, festivals, and the interactions between the spiritual realms and earth-based human beings.

This is the archive which is at risk of being lost because of the modernity and inferiority complex of a black person, which is caused by colonialism and neo-colonialism. This archive is the life of a black person. It is this archive that makes a black person. Therefore, its continued attrition is creating an African black zombie or ghost who is no longer black but not even white, as he or she yearns to be. This Fanonian condition in which the black person finds himself is described by UKEssays (2018) as follows: the black man is constantly trying, but never fully succeeding, to be white and to assimilate into the white man's world. A black man who believes himself to be equal to the white man and shuns his own people would forever be an outsider to both groups. He could never fit in with either side. He would never gain acceptance from whites, and he would be ridiculed by blacks for trying to evolve. In other words, the loss of the ritual African archive, as Falola (2017, p. 703) describes it, leads to the existence of Africans without identity, Africans without an archive to talk about. One may even go a step further and argue that all the academic noise about the repatriation of a migrated colonial archive is a misplaced call for a black archivist, who in fact should be calling for the recuperation of the African ritual archive.

Independent structures for community archives

The formation of community archives is a structure that is recommended in this book as a force that indigenous communities can use to archive their traditions, cultures, and history, among others. One of the core attributes of community archives is their perceived independence, even though there are some that are inspired and sponsored by mainstream archives. Those not fully independent are operating at arm's length from the archival mainstream and academic institutions. The importance of community independence is motivated by the fact that "community archives can be seen as a form of political protest in that it is an attempt to seize the means by which history is written and correct or amend dominant stories about the past." Hence the thought that this can be only achieved if they are independent from the monopolisers of history making such as mainstream archives (Caswell, Harter & Jules 2017, p. 2). This is what makes them community archives in the first place. Flinn, Stevens and Shepherd (2009, p. 73) argue that the

> defining characteristic of community archives is the active participation of a community in documenting and making accessible the history of their particular group and/or locality on their own terms. These terms range from complete autonomy from the 'mainstream' to the delegation of the custody and preservation of their materials to public-sector archivists and a wide range of options in between.

However, independence usually goes hand in hand with financial stability. Baker and Collins (2017, p. 479) note that one of the challenges "concerns the ability to sustain community archives as autonomous ventures, using resources that are independent of public funds." These same sentiments are echoed by Zavala, Migoni, Caswell, Geraci and Cifor (2017, p.209), who observe in their research on community archiving that "funding, personnel, space, and access to other resources were limited across organisations, constraining their work, and presenting perhaps the most significant challenge to their long-term sustainability." Jules (2018) states that

> money, labor, and time have always been identified as the main barriers to progress, whether it is for safe preservation, keeping the building open, hiring staff, maintaining and growing the collections, doing preservation or outreach, or providing broader access to materials.

Without financial stability, the quest for community archives to maintain their independence becomes a precarious situation that can be referred to as a sword of Damocles.

In most cases, the funders expect their programme themes to take centre stage. One can then ask whether community archives can be really independent. Are they able to get together enough resources to conduct their work? Are they able to get adequate support from their communities in terms of financial resources? These questions are very important in the sense that independence can be difficult to achieve without stable financial resources. It also becomes an ideological challenge for the community archives to rely on universities and mainstream heritage centres in the sense that what they are trying to address and correct is a result of these Eurocentric institutions. Caswell et al. (2017, p. 1) discuss the paradox faced by community archives seeking to tell the stories of previously marginalised peoples, noting that "such organisations are frequently created in response to minoritised communities being shut out of dominant historical narratives created by mainstream memory institutions." So, for them to now rely on mainstream memory institutions becomes contradictory. As Jules (2018) argues, it is a dire situation for community archives in such a position of having to rely on mainstream organisations for funding:

It must be recognised that academic institutions have historically promoted Eurocentric, extractive, and systemically racist approaches to scholarship and research, amounting to historical trauma for the very communities these institutions now seek to engage. We must resist these ideas. Therefore, we believe libraries, archives, special collections, or museums based at academic institutions can support and collaborate on this work, but they are seldom suited to lead this work. Instead, grant funders should seek partnerships led by trusted community organisations or community-based archives.

Knowledge of the past needs to be produced within and outside universities and mainstream archives (Field, 2008). Therefore, these once-marginalised communities need to think beyond mainstream archives as they try to document their stories. Even without financial support from the mainstream archives, resources can be pulled from within the communities and voluntary work can be encouraged. Different communities in different communal places can come up with their own community archives that document their traditions and cultures. Bhebhe (2022, p. 105) advocates for an apolitical, independent commission that is not beholden to those in power and has a diverse board of directors to oversee national and community archiving in any country. In other words, one of the archival structures being advocated for here is that which is free from interfering with the colonial archive. The colonial archive is preserved, while parallel indigenous community archives are established to tell the stories of black people.

Semi-supported independent indigenous archival structures

From the onset, this book made it clear that it is not subscribing to the golden utopian past and the revulsion of the present or Western ways of knowing, but it is the by-product of all ways of knowing that are accommodative to African epistemologies. Fault lines have been identified in the conventional mainstream archives that have a bearing on the archival documentation of the indigenous groups of people on the African continent and beyond. However, some of these Eurocentric infrastructures have become part of our lives to the extent that it is impractical to do away with them.

The postcolonial government was even using them to deposit their records. That is why some scholars call for their decolonisation so that they become more convenient in accommodating the stories of others. However, in the preceding chapters of this book, we were calling for more than decolonisation. It is recommended that any archival setup in this postcolonial era should accommodate the IKS. This is a fact well noted by Khumalo and Baloyi (2017, p. 10) when they remark that universities, governments, researchers, the private sector, IK practitioners, and other stakeholders can come together to document IK. In addition to that, Khumalo and Baloyi (2017, p. 10) urge for research infrastructures such as laboratories, libraries, archives, and an effective system of information storage, retrieval, and utilisation to be incorporated; as well as appropriate management systems to be incorporated. Ngulube, Masuku and Sigauke (2011, p. 270) call for the establishment of indigenous knowledge centres which will work with the national archives in the preservation of traditional ways of knowing. They argue that "the indigenous knowledge centres are repositories of community knowledge, places where knowledge can grow, and places where two-way cultural learning can occur." They further argue that "as a repository of captured, documented and preserved indigenous knowledge, an IK centre is a place where indigenous culture and knowledge are showcased to the wider community and preserved to pass on to future generations" (Ngulube et al., 2011, p. 270–271).

Community archives are known for their clamour of independence. However, there are cases in which mainstream archives and universities have played a major role in the development of community archives. Community archives such as GALA, the Jewish Digital Archive Project both in South Africa, and the BaTonga Community Museum in Zimbabwe have benefited a lot from mainstream heritage institutions such as the Witwatersrand University for GALA, the South African Museum for the Jewish Digital Archive Project and the National Museum and Monuments of Zimbabwe for the BaTonga Community Museum. Since 2020, the National Archives of Zimbabwe has taken it upon itself to establish community archives in Acturus Mine, Harare Girls High School, Zimbabwe Christian Church, Shabani Mine, Kariba Community Archives and Gwanda Community Archives (National Archives of Zimbabwe 2022). Even though the modus operandi used in establishing these community archives is debatable in terms of the initiation process, the jury is still out on their success, especially in how sustainable they are. Therefore, even though independent community archives may look preferable when it comes to the archiving of the indigenous knowledge, these other archives, supported by mainstream heritage institutions that speak to the decolonised archive, can be a structure to look into. Maina (2012, p. 13) calls for "libraries and other information institutions need to re-examine and reconstruct themselves in ways that take into account non-western epistemologies and worldviews and develop much needed cultural competency in order to undertake traditional knowledge custodianship." Such a spirit of collaboration is explained by Ngara (2019, p. 206), who argues that "in addition, institutions of higher learning may empower certain local people by offering them the requisite formal training and education that allow them to document and preserve their cultural legacies in their respective rural communities." Ngara (2019, p. 206) states that mainstream institutions should "also establish community-based performance centres and community-based indigenous instrument manufacturing industries that are manned by these rural community people who should be working as state employees." In summary, Ngara (2019, p. 205) proffers that "it is the Community-State model (CSM) that local communities may be empowered to promote preservation and a sustainable cultural economy through rural development." Therefore, the once colonised and marginalised black community can think of working with mainstream heritage institutions to tell their stories. The advantage of such a structure is the issue of sustainability.

Online archival structures

The internet and the widespread use of information and communication technologies (ICTs) made it possible for the archive to lose its traditional characteristic of being static and fixed and becoming fluid. Archives can now be stored anywhere by anyone, be it in the cloud or other online platforms. Social networking sites have played a major role in giving the 'other' a voice, as noted by Moon (2016, p. 196) that online social networking sites have allowed the formation of multiple and diverse "narrative connections" between public audiences and cultural heritage collections. Moon (2016, pp. 197–198) argues that "online platforms for digital resource sharing in particular have become popular as collaborative tools for repatriation, cultural revitalization, and large-scale safeguarding and sustainability projects that involve partnerships between various government and academic organizations, community groups, and NGOs." Poorna, Mymoon and Hariharan (2014) list some of the huge national digital databases that preserve traditional knowledge, such as the Traditional Knowledge Digital Library (TKDL) in India, the Korean Traditional Knowledge Portal, the Chinese Traditional Medicine Database System, the BioZula Project of Venuezela and the Ulwazi Programme of Durban.

The inception of the extensive use of ICTs and the internet meant that governments are no longer solely the shapers of the archive. People from the lower levels of society can now also come up with their own archives. This means that even some of the indigenous groups of people whose histories are not preserved in the inherited colonial archive and its postcolonial manifestations can now document their stories, cultures, and traditions using online platforms. Te Awhina Ka'al-Mahuta (2012) mentions that the loss of the Māori language and culture is worrying, hence the use of Tmata Toiere, an online digital repository. The repository is free to access and aims to provide comprehensive information regarding some of the traditional and cultural aspects of the Māori people. Te Awhina Ka'al-Mahuta (2012, p. 107) further describes Tmata Toiere as "a tool for the revitalisation of the Māori language and the preservation of the Māori culture; a digital memory bank of indigenous Māori knowledge; an archive for future generations." Not only community archives but also mainstream institutions are using the internet to provide access to indigenous archives. This is noted by Chowdhurry, Mcleod, Lihoma, Teferra and Wato (2021, p. 2), who argue "that very little research has been undertaken to promote access to the wealth of cultural heritage and government/indigenous information held at various national archives and government institutions in Africa." Furthermore, it was revealed that millions of records and information objects have been digitised at various memory institutions, but these items largely remain inaccessible because of a lack of ICT infrastructure, financial and human resources, and policies.

The United Nations, through its arm of UNESCO, is also venturing into the preservation of indigenous knowledge, especially through the creation of a world-wide online register for intangible heritage. In Zimbabwe, the National Archives of Zimbabwe (NAZ), working with UNESCO and the Department of Arts, collected and transcribed VaRemba of Mberengwa's oral traditions during the Intangible Cultural Heritage (ICH) inventorying workshop in Zvishavane from August 29 to September 2, 2016. The project is detailed by Bhebhe (2019, p. 110), who outlines that

> what was collected were the oral traditions of the *Komba, Dzingiso* and *Bira* traditions of the VaRemba people, and these are defined in the following: *Komba* was used as an initiation ceremony for the VaRemba/VaMwenye girls and women to impart a variety of skills in readiness for marriage. On the other hand, *Dzingiso* is a male initiation practice for the VaRemba for males aged between eight and fifteen years, and it is usually done in winter for three months. *Bira* is a VaRemba/VaMwenye ritual that is meant to bring back the spirit of the dead so as to reunite it with the living family and God. It is worth noting that these cultural practices especially *Dzingiso* (traditional circumcision), are consistently being practised by very few ethnic minority groups in Zimbabwe. These are the VaRemba (mainly found in Mberengwa), the Tsonga (mainly found in Chiredzi) and the Xhosa (mainly found in Ntabazinduna). Hence their being prioritised in documentation initiatives by NAZ and the Department of Arts, Culture and Heritage in 2016.

In South Africa, Moon (2016, p. 199) talks about how the UNESCO Convention for the Safeguarding of the Intangible Cultural Heritage and national policy are manifesting "in the context of eNanda, a collaborative heritage website directed towards safeguarding ICH in Inanda, South Africa." The Ulwazi Programme (2022) describes eNanda as this "interactive site [which] is a never-ending repository for the rich culture and traditions of eNanda (also known as Inanda), a historically unique township on South Africa's eastern seaboard." The Ulwazi Programme (2022) continues to state that this online "site is meant to help preserve memories, traditional heritage and contemporary culture through modern technology, share it with the world and promote it for tourism" and it "is envisaged to become an invaluable resource for researchers and anyone interested in oral history and changing cultural practices."

The importance of these online archival structures is explained again by Moon (2016, pp. 191–192), who observes that "the 2003 UNESCO *Convention for the Safeguarding of the Intangible Cultural Heritage* has increasingly manifest in the form of nationally driven digital heritage projects that utilise participatory methodologies to produce online community-generated archives." Moon (2016, p. 192), writing about these digital projects when they are being run by mainstream heritage institutions, argues that although the collaborative approaches of these projects offer promising new directions, the disadvantage is that some of their implementations are top-down policies, and the application of external value systems associated with UNESCO continues to be problematised.

The use of ICTs and the internet makes it possible to have national databases for what archives hold, including community ones. It is noteworthy that South Africa is already doing that through its National Register for Oral Sources (NAROS) database for oral history sources. NAROS is part of the National Oral History Programme (NOHP) in which it was decided that an online NAROS should be developed in which all oral history sources in the country are indexed. This was meant, among other reasons, to inform interested parties about research conducted on subjects that may be of interest. Bhebhe (2019, p. 269) commends the National Archives and Records Services (NARS) for coming up with NAROS, which has "proved to be a worthwhile exercise as the database tries to index 'all' oral sources about South Africa from different private, communal, and public institutions." Therefore, it is suggested that in the proposed structure, all countries in Africa, under the supervision of the African Union, can come up with online databases that show what they have in their national and community archives, including other heritage centres. After that, the African Union may even think of the African Archival Online Database (AAOD), which also indexes indigenous archives. This proposed AAOD framework is not a new idea per se, as the literature review shows that some scholars like Chowdhurry et al. (2021, p. 2) suggested that Africa needs

> a searchable online catalogue – to be developed and managed by a Pan-African organisation – should link online catalogues/

metadata of African archival documents, indigenous, government and cultural heritage content available in various African institutions and elsewhere in the world. This will ensure that users will be able to discover African indigenous content and government information irrespective of where they are available.

This idea of archival national online databases has a long history and is becoming a prevalent discourse, as some scholars like Maina (2012) narrate how in New Zealand, libraries, community archives, and mainstream heritage institutions are sharing content and metadata using the online Mukurtu platform. Mukurtu (2022) labels the Mukurtu Content Management System as "a grassroots project aiming to empower communities to manage, share, narrate, and exchange their digital heritage in culturally relevant and ethically-minded ways." It allows one to share digital cultural heritage with respect to community protocols, especially when it comes to access (Mukurtu, 2022). The Mukurtu Content Management System also allows one to add multiple community stories as it "provides multiple cultural narratives, traditional knowledge, and diverse sets of protocols, ensuring that you can tell your stories and your history, your way" (Mukurtu, 2022). Therefore, online indigenous archives provide another avenue for previously marginalised peoples to tell their stories.

Conclusion

In this chapter, various types of archival structures were proposed, along with their benefits and drawbacks. The design of any structure by any group of people will undoubtedly be influenced by a variety of factors, including issues of sustainability. Some communities may prefer a fully independent structure, whereas others may prefer a semi-independent structure. Other communities may even prefer to go online and preserve their archives in such spaces. However, it is recommended that, after all is said and done, it should always be the objective of all African governments or the Global South as a whole to revive their ritual archive as defined by Falola (2017). This is significant in the sense that the ritual archive is what defines black people. It is their identity, their way of life.

References

Baker, S. and Collins, J. (2017). Popular music heritage, community archives and the challenge of sustainability. *International Journal of Cultural Studies*, 20(5): 476–491. doi:10.1177/1367877916637150

Battiste, M. and Henderson, J.Y. (2000). *Protecting indigenous knowledge and heritage: a global challenge*. Saskatoon: Purich Publishing.

Bhebhe, S. (2019). *Memorialising minority groups in post-independence Zimbabwe and South Africa: A critical analysis of oral history programme*. PhD thesis, Pretoria: University of South Africa.

Bhebhe, S. (2022). Proposed independent organisational structure for memory institutions in Zimbabwe and South Africa. *Collection and Curation*, 41(3): 101–106. doi:10.1108/CC-05-2021-0017

Caswell, M., Harter, C. and Jules, B. (2017). Diversifying the digital historical record: integrating community archives in national strategies for access to digital cultural heritage. *The Magazine of Digital Library Research*, 23(5/6): 1–6. https://doi.org/10.1045/may2017-caswell

Chowdhurry, G., Mcleod, J., Lihoma, P., Teferra, S. and Wato, R. (2021). Promoting access to indigenous information in Africa: challenges and requirements. *Information Development*, 1–13. doi:10.1177/02666669211048488

Falola, T. (2017). Ritual archive. In A. Afolayan and T. Falola (Eds.), *The Palgrave handbook of African philosophy*, London: Palgrave Macmillan.

Fanon, F. (2001). *The wretched of the earth*, trans. Constance Farrington, Penguin Classics edition, London: Penguin.

Field, S. (2008). Turning up the volume: dialogues about memory create oral histories. *South African Historical Journal*, 60(2): 175–194. doi:10.1080/02582470802416393

Flinn, A., Stevens, M. and Shepherd, E. (2009). Whose memories, whose archives, autonomy and the mainstream. *Archival Science*, 9: 71–86. doi:10.1007/s10502-009-9105-2

Intwasa ARTS Festival koBULAWAYO (2022). About Intwasa Arts Festival koBulawayo. Available at: www.facebook.com/intwasa/about/?ref=page_internal (Accessed 10 August 2022).

Jules, B. (2018). Let the people lead: supporting sustainability versus dependency models for funding community-based archives. Available at: http://medium.com/community-archive/let-the=people-lead-supporting-sustainability-vs-dependency-models-for-funding-community-based-b114948c0e74 (Accessed 10 May 2022).

Khumalo, N.B. and Baloyi, C. (2017). African indigenous knowledge: an underutilised and neglected resource for development. *Library Philosophy and Practice (e-journal)*. 1663. https://digitalcommons.unl.edu/libphilprac/1663 (Accessed 12 July 2022).

Luker, T. (2017). Decolonising archives: indigenous challenges to record keeping in 'Reconciling' settler colonial states. *Australian Feminist Studies*, 32(91/92): 108–125. doi:10.1080/08164649.2017.1357011

Magoqwana, B. (2021). Gendering social science: Ukubuyiswa of maternal legacies of knowledge for balanced social sciences studies in South Africa. In B. Muthien and J. Bam (Eds.), *Rethinking Africa: indigenous women re-interpret Southern Africa's pasts*, Pretoria: Fanele Imprint, pp. 87–102.

Maina, C.K. (2012). Traditional knowledge management and preservation: intersections with Library and Information Science. *The International Information & Library Review*, 44: 13–27.

Maluleka, J.R. (2017). *Acquisition, transfer and preservation of indigenous knowledge by traditional healers in the Limpopo province of South Africa*. PhD thesis, Pretoria, University of South Africa.

Marschall, S. (2014). eNanda online: sharing Zulu cultural heritage on the Internet. *International Journal of Intangible Heritage*, 9: 120–133.

Masuku, M. and Pasipamire, N. (2014). Going against the grain: questioning the role of archivists and librarians in the documentation and preservation of indigenous knowledge. *ESARBICA Journal*, 33: 117–130.

Moon, J. (2016). Uploading Matepe: online learning, sustainability and repatriation in Northeastern Zimbabwe. H. Klisala (Ed.), *Applied ethnomusicology in institutional policy and practice*, Helsinki: Studies across Disciplines in the Humanities and Social Sciences, p. 190–209. Available at: https://core.ac.uk/display/78562665 (Accessed 15 June 2022).

Mukurtu Website. (2022). *Our Mission*. Available at: https://mukurtu.org/about/ (Accessed 10 May 2022).

Ngara, R. (2019). *Kayanda musical arts for the installation of Shangwe chiefs: an epistemological, gendered, symbolic, interpretive, community–state model for sustaining tangible and intangible heritage in Zimbabwe*. PhD thesis, Pretoria: University of Pretoria. Available at: https://repository.up.ac.za/handle/2263/72659 (Accessed 12 January 2022).

Ngoepe, M. (2022). Neither prelegal nor nonlegal: Oral memory in troubled times. *HTS Teologiese Studies/Theological Studies*, 78(3): a7533. Available at: https://doi.org/10.4102/hts.v78i3.7533 (Accessed 12 August 2022).

Ngoepe, M. and Setumu, T. (2016). Converting oral narratives into written literature: lessons learnt from heritage projects undertaken in the Makgabeng area, Limpopo, South Africa. *Mousaion*, 34(4): 15–29.

Ngulube, P., Masuku, M. and Sigauke, T. (2011). The role of archives in preserving indigenous knowledge systems in Zimbabwe: is (re) inventing themselves the answer? *ESARBICA Journal*, 30: 261–278.

Onyima, B.N. (2016). Nigerian cultural heritage: preservation, challenges and prospects. *Ogirisi: A New Journal of African Studies*, 12: 273–292. http://dx.doi.org/10.4314/og.v12i 1.15

Poorna, R, Mymoon, M. and Hariharan, A. (2014). Preservation and protection of traditional knowledge – diverse documentation initiatives across the globe. *Current Science*, 107(8): 1240–1246.

Rahmam, F. and Letlora, P.S. (2018). Cultural preservation: rediscovering the endangered oral tradition of Maluku. *Advances in Language and Literary Studies*, 9(2): 91–97. http://dx.doi.org/10.7575/aiac.alls.v.9n.2p.91

Setumu, T. (2015). Inclusion of rural communities in national archival and records system: a case study of Blouberg-Makgabeng-Senwabarwana area. *Journal of South African Society of Archivists*, 48: 34–44.

Setumu, T. (2016). Africa in the Arts (visual, performance, digital, music): a case study of Blouberg-Makgabeng-Senwabarwana (BMS) Festivals Project. Paper presented at the UNISA School of Arts Triennial Conference: Exploring the African continent through the Arts: re-mapping, re-thinking, re-imagining Africa. 14–15 September, Pretoria.

Te Awhina Ka'al – Mahuta, R. (2012). Digital technology: contemporary methods for the dissemination of ancient knowledge. The use of digital technology in the preservation of Māori song. *Te Kaharoa*, (5) Special Edition: 99–108. Available at: www.tekaharoa.com/index.php/tekaharoa/article/view/98/92 (Accessed 10 May 2022).

Ulwazi Programme. (2022). *eNanda.co.za launches!* Available at: www.ukessays.com/essays/english-literature/black-skin-white-masks-by-frantz-fanon-english-literature-essay.php?vref=1 (Accessed 18 April 2022).

Zavala, J., Migoni, A.A., Caswell, M., Geraci, N. and Cifor, M. (2017). A process where we're all at the table: community archives challenging dominant modes of archival practice. *Archives and Manuscripts*, 45(3): 202–215. doi:10.1080/01576895.2017.1377088

Epilogue
Reflections and reflexivity

This book questioned and contested the Western orthodoxy of a record through examples such as murals, rock art paintings, and oral memory, especially family praises, and nomenclatures as indigenous archives. It addressed the lamentation by Harris (2000) that the work of deconstructing the dominant orthodoxy of building archival praxis rooted in African realities and traditions remains to be done. With the example of oral memory given, history is no longer limited to the powerful, famous, rich, and literate. Now, history can give us a much more inclusive, and, one hopes, accurate picture of the past. However, it should always be noted that even in critical emancipation, there can be elitism as Bhebhe and Ngoepe (2021) argue. For example, with oral traditions, the focus may still be on the lives and activities of great men, that is, kings and chiefs, with little to say about the everyday aspects of societies. In South Africa and Zimbabwe, for example, this has been perpetuated by the governing parties, the African National Congress, and the ZANU-PF, respectively. When recording oral histories, only stories of those who waged liberation struggles are captured and stories of heroes in other sectors of society such as sports are overlooked. Hence, Matshotshwane and Ngoepe (2022) indicate that the Gauteng Provincial Archives rather opted to collect memories of sports heroes to close the perceived gap.

The discussion in this book brought forth the issue of oral history as a method and oral history happening in its natural setting. As a method, the researcher walks around with a tape recorder or any form of recording equipment, interviewing people. This produces oral history documents in a new format such as digital video and camera, just as audio is converted into text transcript. We consider oral history to be original when it occurs in its natural

DOI: 10.4324/9781003277989-8

setting and people have a conversation narrating their stories rather than somebody recording a story about them. Even written archives can cement officially sanctioned narratives in concrete. As Wrong (2021) would attest, even with a solidified cement, counter narratives, complexities, and nuances get lost in the heritage and cultural organisations, consciously and unconsciously so.

The omission, neglect, and destruction of African epistemologies in epistemology spaces have been the motivation behind writing this book. Heritage mainstream or conventional spaces found in Africa are still replete with Eurocentric epistemologies. In order to address this, almost all the African countries embarked on decolonisation programmes when they got their independence. However, with achievements here and there, nothing much has been done to change the prevalent Eurocentric epistemologies which are still dominant in Africa. Archives, museums, and other heritage spaces are still more Eurocentric in their approach despite patches of decolonisation here and there. Even though imperial forces are always blamed for this status quo, Africans themselves, including its intelligentsia, have not done much in practical terms to address this epistemic injustice faced by the continent. This has led to the reasoning that maybe these decolonisation mantras are just theoretical noises, academic jamborees, and slogan trumpeting that are failing to be practically implemented.

One does not deny that much has been written academically and otherwise on Africanisation, decolonisation and indigenisation, but on the ground, Eurocentric epistemologies still stands tall in all African spaces. Hence, the thrust of this book to try to offer practical solutions to the demonisation of African epistemologies. Some of the practical solutions proffered are the encouragement of the formation of counter archives that take into consideration the importance of indigenous archives. Counter archiving is the phenomenon that has been able to challenge the mainstream archives by offering the 'others' who are usually omitted in the national historiography to document their stories. The example of the LGBTI community with the formation of the Gay and Lesbian Memory in Action Archive in South Africa was used as a case study in this book to show how colonial archives can be decolonised. Instead of attempting to change the colonial archives by removing some of the records that speak to the imperialists and adding those that are meant to preserve African voices, the continent can just

Epilogue: reflections and reflexivity 139

opt for community archives. Other examples such as the Avuxeni Community Museum in Zimbabwe and Makgabeng Rock Art Community Project in South Africa, and the Comrades Marathon Association were highlighted and mentioned in this book. These case studies are giving hope of a possibility that a colonial archive can be decolonised, while community archives that speak to the indigeneity of African people are created, promoted, and used. This may also help that more and more people would use archives, as there has been lamentation from various scholars such as Ngulube, Ngoepe, Saurombe and Chaterera (2017), Ngoepe and Ngulube (2011), and Venson, Ngoepe and Ngulube (2014).

The dilemma and sometimes the hypocrisy of decolonisation of heritage institutions have been that it tends to create a situation where African ways of knowing are portrayed as playing second fiddle to Eurocentric epistemologies. The example that comes to mind is that some heritage decolonists are advocating for the inclusion of African ways of knowing in Eurocentric heritage institutions. It should be noted that African epistemologies have existed and survived for a long time, independent from Western ways of knowing. They should never be used as a way of filling gaps in conventional archives, as has been suggested by others. Therefore, what should be of priority for the heritage decolonists is the revival of the systems that are used to preserve the African ways of knowing, for example, the promotion of the *uMakhulu* concept (this concept is positioned on the role that was being played by our African grandmothers in bringing up their grandchildren). This *uMakhulu* concept, as explained by Magoqwana (2021, p. 8), as "positions *uMakhulu* as an institution of knowledge that transfers not only 'history' through *iintsomi* (folktales), but also as a body of indigenous knowledge that stores, transfers and disseminates knowledge and values." Therefore, the revival of such African institutions that face obliteration due to Western influences and the inferiority complex of the Africans themselves should be encouraged.

In this book, in order to support the promotion of such African institutions, a naturally fluid indigenous archival structure was proposed. These are structures that endeavour to maintain the traditional setup of how our African societies have preserved their knowledge since time immemorial. Other interesting decolonial programmes that are being adopted by institutions of learning such as the Rhodes University and the University of Cape Town need to be encouraged. These two institutions are decolonising the archives by using the Five Hundred Years Archive (FHYA) project to draw attention to the underserved areas of southern Africa's past, particularly the time before European colonialism (Fengu, 2022). The purpose of FHYA is to support

> historical research into these neglected eras and to encourage the digitisation and the sharing of resources across a network of institutions. It also aims to build a public community of users who are passionate about southern African history and who are interested in the complex forces which shape that history over time.
>
> (Five Hundred Years Archive, 2022)

The FHYA also endeavours to break with inherited colonial orientations and expectations, as it is an opportunity to build new kinds of archives that are open to new epistemological futures (Archive and Public Culture, 2022). Therefore, such archival programmes should be encouraged as a way of bringing to the fore the African epistemologies and correcting biases and distortions in the official archives and other sources. Indigenous archives are also crucial because they can contribute to solutions to solving weird problems. They can also help open up new areas of inquiry. As cultural institutions such as museums and archives are thinly spread in Africa due to underfunding and poor maintenance not refreshed since colonial time, and new ones disappear, indigenous archives such as murals and rock art paintings can serve as counter archives and trigger tourism, which will be an essential part of any visit. The recognition of murals, family praises, nomenclature, and rock art paintings as archives offers an opportunity for archives in alternative spaces similar to the concept of the archival threshold which according to Lowry (n.d.) is rooted in a seventeenth-century archival law for trust in public institutions and officers.

Post-coloniality and post-colonial scholars have shown the existence of African epistemologies and ontologies and how imperialism and colonialism have been at the forefront in the unprecedented epistemic onslaught of this knowledge. The harm associated with the sidelining of indigenous archives has taken regions such as Africa many centuries back. It is now time for African cultural reclamation by recalling the pasts through indigenous archives. This may help to restore the identities of many Africans whose voices are missing from the mainstream archival institutions. It may also lead to the survival of indigenous knowledge and the stimulation of the ongoing work of decolonisation and (re)Africanisation. Failure by African archivists to take the lead in decolonisation and (re)Africanisation may lead to indigenous archives being usurped and the reduction of Africans to what Sisante (2012) calls gatecrashers, while the usurpers are elevated to gatekeepers. As a result of externalisation through commercialisation, indigenous archives might lose its provenance in the hands of the gatecrashers who metamorphose into gatekeepers. The survival of the indigenous African archive will only be through its use in its natural setting. Archivists should push for the continuous use and performance of the indigenous African archive through its documentation and domestication in archival repositories. There is also a need to rethink how indigenous archives can be copyrighted without violating its communal use vis-à-vis commercialisation. Indigenous archives have the potential to drive future archives, especially at individual, family, and community level to archive memories from different sources. This is already evident from the engaged scholarship project by the Gauteng Provincial Archives Repository, in collaboration with the University of South Africa, to preserve memories of previously marginalised athletes whose voices are missing from the archives (Matshotshwane & Ngoepe, 2022). Preliminary results of the project suggest that athletes' self-stored memories are mostly displayed in their living rooms, on their walls and on television stands at their homes. The muted voices in the form of indigenous archives need to be unmuted through removal from their nadir position and placed in the original prevalent position they were in during the precolonial period. Indigenous archives are also crucial because they can contribute solutions to grand societal challenges.

References

Archive and Public Culture, (2022). The Five Hundred Years Archive. Available at: www.apc.uct.ac.za/apc/research/projects/five-hundred-year-archive (Accessed 14 July 2022).

Bhebhe, S. and Ngoepe, M. (2021). Elitism in critical emancipatory paradigm: national archival oral history collection in Zimbabwe and South Africa. *Archival Science*, 21: 155–172.
Fengu, M. (2022). Rhodes, UCT partner to decolonise historical archives. *City Press Newspaper*, 30 August. Available at: www.news24.com/citypress/news/rhodes-uct-partner-to-decolonise-historical-archives-20220830 (1 September 2022).
Five Hundred Years Archive. (2022). *Welcome*. Available at: https://fhya.org/ (Accessed 30 August 2022).
Harris, V. (2000). *Exploring archives: an introduction to archival ideas and practice in South Africa*. 2nd ed. Pretoria: National Archives of South Africa.
Lowry, J. (n.d.). The inverted archive: thresholds, authenticity and the demos.
Magoqwana, B. (2021). Gendering social science: Ukubuyiswa of maternal legacies of knowledge for balanced social sciences studies in South Africa. In B. Muthien and J. Bam (Eds.), *Rethinking Africa: indigenous women re-interpret Southern Africa's Pasts*. Pretoria: Fanele Imprint, pp. 87–102.
Matshotshwane, J. and Ngoepe, M. (2022). Transcending invisible lanes through inclusion of sports memories in archival system in South Africa. *HTS Teologiese Studies/Theological Studies*, 78(3): 6.
Ngoepe, M. and Ngulube, P. (2011). Assessing the extent to which the National Archives and Records Services of South Africa has fulfilled its mandate of taking the archives to the people. *Innovation: Journal of Appropriate Librarianship and Information Work in Southern Africa*, 42: 3–22.
Ngulube, P., Ngoepe, M., Saurombe, N. and Chaterera, F. (2017). Towards a uniform strategy for taking archives to the people in South Africa. *ESARBICA Journal*, 36: 75–93.
Sisante, S. (2012). The media and Africa's on-going quest for a true humanity: a Bikoian approach. *Communitas*, 17: 59–74.
Venson, S., Ngoepe, M. and Ngulube, P. (2014). The role of archives in national development in selected countries in the East and Southern Africa Regional Branch of the International Council on Archives region. *Innovation: Journal of Appropriate Librarianship and Information Work in Southern Africa*, 48(1): 46–68.
Wrong, M. (2021). *Do not disturb: the story of a political murder and an African regime gone bad*. London: HarperCollins Publishers.

Index

Note: Endnotes are indicated by the page number followed by "n" and the note number e.g., 35n1 refers to note 1 on page 35. Page numbers in *italic* refers to Figures.

academic institutions, racist approaches 127
Africa: as dehumanised 41; seen as having no history 42, 43
African Archival Online Database (AAOD) proposal 132
African archivists 8, 40, 44, 54, 58; lack of 54
African communities: land ownership 84; organisation of societies 83
African illiteracy from a Western point of viewpoint 43
African indigenous law in property 84
African management systems 106
African Rock Art Digital Archive (SARADA) 33, 35n2, 76
African understanding of shared resources 9
Africanisation and re-Africanisation 10, 42; archives 6–7; defined 41–2; of homophobia 102
Africa's rich cultural and intellectual traditions denied 39, 40, 41
Afrocentric perspective, emphasis on people 3
Alexandra Township 24
ANC and other liberation movement archives 102
ancestors' responsibility to preserve knowledge 120
ancestral tourism 32, 34
Ancestral Voices project 33, 35n1
anti-LGBTI: environment 104; legislation 103
apartheid: as an ideology 50; leaders' words recorded 49; police photographs of LGBTI individuals 104
archival: activism 54; decolonization 53; holdings as a voice 49; legislation 2; structure, online 129–33; system that silenced African voices 40; theory, evolving and mutating 46
Archival Platform 109, 113
archives 5, 13, 43, 44, 46, 49; African 41, 42–8, 58, 122; apartheid archive 50; colonial exclusion of natives 3, 45, 52; colonialism and apartheid 39, 54; 'Contemporary' 110–11; definition 12, 13, 24; destruction by colonial state officials 52; empire's 48–51; Eurocentric 42, 47–8, 138; exploitation by outsiders 82; and imperialism 10; inclusive 2, 10, 11; liberation movement 102; mistrust of state and institutional archives 119;

144 *Index*

official 56, 96; originals left intact 53, 55, 127; postcolonial 51; to preserve memory 45; at risk of being lost 45, 124; ritual 124; total 10; Western and African views 4, 11–12, 53; *see also* community archives, indigenous archives
'Archiving Gala' collection 107
artificial intelligence technologies 32
Asian countries' indigenous knowledge systems 8–9
athletes, missing voices 141
Australia, community-centric archive 13
authentication 69–71, 79; memory 66; of murals 75–6; witness testimony 70, 72–3

Baartman, Sarah, remains of 50
Bahananwa 22, 74
Bantu Administration Act (1927) 84
Bantu-speaking people 21; rock art paintings 22, *22*
Batlhaloga people 20
Battle of the Blood River 50
Bhebhe clan 17
Biko, Steve 88
black people's desire to become white 124
black South African women 12–13
blockchain technology 4, 6, 66, 72, 73
Blouberg-MakgabengSenwabarwana (BMS) arts and culture festival 123
Boer Republic 22–3
Botswana 74, 86
bottom-up approach 96
Bow (Leeroy Spinx Brittain) 25, 26, 27, 29
Bulawayo 26, 27

Canada: archives 2–3, 10, 55; oral tradition as evidence 73, 78; settlement of indigenous lands 40; Truth and Reconciliation 2
Cape Town Archives Repository 39
case studies: Avuxeni Community Museum 95; lesbian, gay, bisexual, transgender, and intersex (LGBTI) community 95; Makgabeng Rock Art Community Project 95
chieftaincy, histories expressed in culture 15
children: with English names 124; raising to be responsible adults 44
Christian Nationalist ideology 104
clan names 15, 18
colonial governments: deprived people of land 83, 84, 85; as record-keepers 48; view of Africans 4, 39
colonial imposition of its values 8
colonisation, corrosive effects of 123–4
colonisers carved up land using documents 83, 85
community archives 54, 98, 139; addressing historical omissions 96; benefit from mainstream heritage institutions 128; as centres of revolution 97; characteristics of 125; collective and consensus 106; concept of 96; designation 96; domination by oral records and artefacts 107; independence of 125–7, 128, 129; philosophy behind 96–100, 107; use of digital tools 97
Comrades Marathon 29, *30*
constitutions, unwritten 106
Copyleft 91–2; applicability to indigenous archives 93; definition 91; free availability 91
Copyright 89–91; community ownership 89; eligibility for 89; exclusion of indigenous

archives 89; exemption from 89; negotiating royalties 90
Copyright and Neighbouring Rights Act of Zimbabwe 90–1, 92, 93
cultural festivals 72, 73, 122–3

Deaf LGBTI oral history project 109
deaf MSM (Men who have Sex with Men) 109
decolonisation: archives 1, 4, 40, 51–7; of collection-related terms and names 53; definition 40; in the Gay and Lesbian Memory in Action 102–3; sceptics 41
derogatory colonial names 53
displacement of families 85

elitism 4–5, 34, 111, 137
eNanda, collaborative heritage website 131
Eswatini Kingdom 18
ethical principles 67–8
Eurocentric infrastructures, some as part of life 127
European epistemologies as universal 'truths' 40–1
extended archives 13, 23, 24, 32, 138; murals as 28

Facebook 98
family praises 13, 14–15, 16, 17; tracing family tree 14–15
#FeesMustFall 96, 109
Five Hundred Years Archive (FHYA) project 140
folklore 139: definition 90; owners to licence their work for royalties 87
forgetfulness 66, 69
Freedom Charter, two versions of 75

GaRankuwa township name 74
gatekeepers and gate-crashers 58, 83, 85, 97

Gauteng Provincial Archives 137, 141
Gay and Lesbian Memory in Action (GALA) 103–4, 110, 112; archive 95, 96, 107–9, 112; and the needs of LGBTI people with disabilities 110; oral history projects 109; organisational structure 105; safe meeting place 112; stories of LGBTI communities 111; at the University of the Witwatersrand 112; website 109; work of 113; youth 110
Gay and Lesbian Organisation of the Witwatersrand (GLOW) 108
Gay Association of South Africa (GASA) 108
Gays and Lesbians of Zimbabwe (GALZ) 108
Gaza Trust 98, 99
Ghana 52
Google Connect 32–3
Google Maps applications 31–2
grandfathers' names 19
Great Limpopo Transfrontier Conservation Area 99
Gukurahundi massacre mural 27

halls of honour 29, 30
Holy Trinity Catholic Church, Braamfontein 110
homosexuality in Africa 102, 103; homophobia 108

identity, loss of 9
iintsomi (folktales) 139
indigenous archives 1, 6, 79, 86–9; ambiguous service agreements 92–3; custodians of 67, 68; fluid nature of 89, 119–25; protection of 67–9; reconstructing 10; and technology 29–33; unclear ownership 82; and written records, can intersect 69
inclusive archives 2, 10, 11
inclusive community based approach 2

indigenous knowledge systems (IKS) 8, 9, 86; in Asian countries 8–9; categorised as irrational and primitive 47; conversion from oral to paper or digital 30, 31; inventions from 87; lack of protection 86–7; protection of 82–3, 87, 121; showcasing 128
indigenous legal and political systems, overwriting by Europeans 40
indigenous memory practices 4
indigenous people: of Australia 3; mistrust of state and institutional archives 119; views different from Western 3
indigenous schools established, experimental 121
Indonesia 121; sacred chant 121
initiation to adulthood 99, 131
Intangible Cultural Heritage (ICH) 122, 131
intellectual property law 89
internet and use of information and communication technologies (ICTs) 129, 130, 132

KARA Heritage Institute, Pretoria 25
Khoisan people 21, 22; rock art paintings 22
kings: deposing of 85; who opposed white governments 68

Land Act (1913) 84
land deprivation 84
land ownership 83, 84, 85; black people buying back their own 16
land resources 83–6; shared and free movement 84, 85
laws 77–9, 89
Lekganyane, Engenas 88
lesbian, gay, bisexual, transgender, and intersex (LGBTI) 96, 104: activism in South Africa 108; archives 103, 104; communities 103; material from organisations and campaigns 107; support for 110
Letlamoreng Dam murals 23–4, 68, 75
liberation freedom fighters 53
Limpopo province 8, 15, 21
Livingstone, David 82
Lobengula, King 25, *27*
local government authorities as custodians of heritage 85

Mabotja family 17
Mai 68 55
Makgabeng area 18, 22
Makgabeng Community Rock Art Heritage project 98, 99
Makgabeng Mountains 15, 84
Makgabeng paintings, free access 77
Makhuba, Mbuyiswa 39, 58–9n1
Malawi 86
Malebogo boer war 22
Malebogo nation, origins of 74
Mamabolo, Ludwick 14
Māori: indigenous archives of 122; language and culture, loss of 130; use of Tmata Toiere, online digital repository 130
marginalised people 39, 96
Matopo National Park 22
Mayibuye Centre, University of the Western Cape 102
Mberengwa's oral traditions 131
medicine men 17, 53, 102
memories 44; considered as records 13; of major African Independent Churches 50; of people in power 34; reliable 69; shared 9; unreliability of 65, 66
Memory of the World 9
Mexico mural 27, *28*
Mfecane 17, 84
Mhlongo 17
mining companies in South Africa 9
minutes of meetings 69
Mogalakwena River 19–20

Index 147

Mogana 19
"mpogo" ritual prayer song 88
muralists (Bow) 25, 26, 27, 29
murals 23–9; authentication 75–6; Barolong kings 24, *24*; defaced, vandalism 75; as extended archives 28; Gukurahundi massacres 27; of KwaZulu-Natal kings 75; of Letlamoreng Dam 23–4, 68, 75; mayors of eThekwini *25*, 76; in Mexico 27, *28*; transformed from records 69; of Zulu kings 25, *26*
museums 5, 75, 99, 102
music 44, 72
Mzilikazi, King 17

Namibia 86; archives 49; Culture and Heritage Council 86; loss of property 49
naming practices 18–19; to trace genealogy 19
National Archives and Records Services (NARS) 89, 132
National Archives and Records Service of South Africa Act 78, 87
National Archives of South Africa 75
National Archives of Zimbabwe (NAZ) 1, 100; working with UNESCO 131
National Coalition for Gay & Lesbian Equality (NCGLE) 108
national digital databases 130
National Heritage and Cultural Studies Centre (NAHECS) 102
National Heritage Acts 78–9
National Oral History Programme (NOHP) 132
National Register for Oral Sources (NAROS) database 132
Ndebele 20–1, 26, 27, *27*, 44, 106
Nelson Mandela Foundation 97
New Zealand 133
Ngoepe, Sankobela 16
Ngoyi's keynote speech 50
nomenclature 18–21, 74

Northern Sotho: paintings 23; proverb 67; word of king 67

oral archive as a living museum 43
oral history 1, 3–4, 16; categories 70; in community archives 100–1; documents in a new format 137; fluidity of 71; leading to community resilience 101; lending confidence to marginalised communities 100; music 72; as non-public record 78; as records 71; witnesses of 70
oral memory 13–18; more than one version 88–9; pushed to the periphery 48
oral traditions (proverbs, riddles, folktales) 43, 46; missing out on making a living from 92
orality 13–18; authenticating 71–5; conversion to recorded form 14; false information 73–4; projects through technology 33; public announcements 72; questioning agenda 73; two versions, one story 74–5
organisational structure of indigenous African systems 105
Out in Africa Film Festival 107
ownership transferred to a cultural institution 92

patents: to protect indigenous knowledge 87; registering without involving the owners 92–3
photographs 71–2, 104
place names 19–20
post-independence communities 3
praise poems 14, 15, 16, 17, 18, 73; as genealogical research 73
pre-colonial practices, reservoirs of knowledge 44
Promotion of Access to Information Act 89
proverb 67
public domain 88, 89, 91

public holidays in South Africa 50

racism, scientific 50
racist language and ideology 53
records: biases in 74; definition 12, 33–4; digitised but inaccessible 130; manipulation of 65; of persons previously classified as non-white 49; showing how to rule the 'native,' 49; trustworthiness of 69–70; Western and African 9
Rhodes Must Fall movement 54
rock art painting: authentication 76–7; damage to 76, 77; digitised 76; experts 77; not declared as heritage sites 90; information and communication 21–3; in law 79; of Makgabeng 85, 87, 99–100; preserving 76–7, 85; projects 33, 35n2; in Zimbabwe 22
rock art sites 22; ownership of land 85, 87; used for ritual ceremonies 99
royalties of 88, 87, 90

same-sex relationships 102
San people 23, 101; possible extinction of 101; rock art paintings *21*, 23
sangomas (traditional healers) 102
Seketa Lebogo, King 22–3
Seychelles 86
social networking sites 98, 129
South Africa: apartheid regime 101; copyright law 93; diversity and richness of heritage 11; independence 52; post-apartheid 9; transition to democracy 10–11
South African Heritage Resource Agency 90
South African History Archives (SAHA) 89, 102

South Sudan 52
Southern African Development Community (SADC) region 86
speeches made by African nationalists 49, 50
spirit medium 25
Steve Biko Foundation 88
story cloths 12–13
surnames 15, 17, 74

taboos 67–8
territory demarcation, refusal 22–3
testimonies of the liberation struggle 95
top-down policies 132
total archives 10
tourism 32, 34
traditional African courts ("edale") 106
Traditional Environmental Knowledge (TEK) 101
Traditional Healers Association of Namibia 86
Tsonga people 99
Tso-ro-tso San Development Trust 101
Tumbale 17

Ubuntu (Humanity) 9
Ulwazi Programme 131
umaKhulu concept 46, 121, 139
United Nations Declaration on the Rights of Indigenous Peoples (UNDRIP) 2, 79
United Nations Educational, Scientific and Cultural Organization (UNESCO) 9, 23; Convention for the Safeguarding of Intangible Cultural Heritage 131, 132; preservation of indigenous knowledge 130–1
University of Zimbabwe's African Languages Research Institute 101

vandalism 75, 77
VaRemba people 131
Victoria Falls 1, 82
voices of minorities and side-lined 49

witness testimony 70, 72–3
Wits School of Rock Art 99
Wits University, History Workshop 102
women involved in the liberation struggle 97

world-wide online register for intangible heritage 130–1

Xhosa tribe's folklore song Mbube 87

Zimbabwe: copyright law 93; independence 52; liberation struggle 20–1; murals 25; praises 17; rock art paintings 22
Zion Christian Church (ZCC) 50, 87, 88

For Product Safety Concerns and Information please contact our EU representative GPSR@taylorandfrancis.com
Taylor & Francis Verlag GmbH, Kaufingerstraße 24, 80331 München, Germany

www.ingramcontent.com/pod-product-compliance
Lightning Source LLC
Chambersburg PA
CBHW051749230426
43670CB00012B/2208